# What Else Can Central B

Geneva Reports on the World Economy 18

**International Center for Monetary and Banking Studies (ICMB)**
International Center for Monetary and Banking Studies
2, Chemin Eugène-Rigot
1202 Geneva
Switzerland

Tel: (41 22) 734 9548
Fax: (41 22) 733 3853
Web: www.icmb.ch

© 2016 International Center for Monetary and Banking Studies

**Centre for Economic Policy Research**
Centre for Economic Policy Research
33 Great Sutton Street
London  EC1V 0DX
UK

Tel: +44 (20) 7183 8801
Fax: +44 (20) 7183 8820
Email: cepr@cepr.org
Web: www.cepr.org

ISBN: 978-0-9954701-1-8

# What Else Can Central Banks Do?

Geneva Reports on the World Economy 18

**Laurence Ball**
Johns Hopkins University

**Joseph Gagnon**
Peterson Institute for International Economics

**Patrick Honohan**
Trinity College Dublin, CEPR and Peterson Institute for International Economics

**Signe Krogstrup**
Peterson Institute for International Economics

ICMB  INTERNATIONAL CENTER FOR MONETARY AND BANKING STUDIES
CIMB  CENTRE INTERNATIONAL D'ETUDES MONETAIRES ET BANCAIRES

CEPR PRESS

## The International Center for Monetary and Banking Studies (ICMB)

The International Center for Monetary and Banking Studies (ICMB) was created in 1973 as an independent, non-profit foundation. It is associated with Geneva's Graduate Institute of International and Development Studies. Its aim is to foster exchanges of views between the financial sector, central banks and academics on issues of common interest. It is financed through grants from banks, financial institutions and central banks. The Center sponsors international conferences, public lectures, original research and publications. In association with CEPR, the Center has published the Geneva Reports on the World Economy since 1999. These reports attract considerable interest among practitioners, policymakers and scholars.

ICMB is non-partisan and does not take any view on policy. Its publications, including the present report, reflect the opinions of the authors, not of ICMB or any of its sponsoring institutions. The President of the Foundation Board is Thomas Jordan and the Director is Charles Wyplosz.

## Centre for Economic Policy Research (CEPR)

The Centre for Economic Policy Research (CEPR) is a network of over 1,000 research economists based mostly in European universities. The Centre's goal is twofold: to promote world-class research, and to get the policy-relevant results into the hands of key decision-makers.

CEPR's guiding principle is 'Research excellence with policy relevance'.

A registered charity since it was founded in 1983, CEPR is independent of all public and private interest groups. It takes no institutional stand on economic policy matters and its core funding comes from its Institutional Members and sales of publications. Because it draws on such a large network of researchers, its output reflects a broad spectrum of individual viewpoints as well as perspectives drawn from civil society.

CEPR research may include views on policy, but the Trustees of the Centre do not give prior review to its publications. The opinions expressed in this report are those of the authors and not those of CEPR.

| | |
|---|---|
| Chair of the Board | Sir Charlie Bean |
| Founder and Honorary President | Richard Portes |
| President | Richard Baldwin |
| Research Director | Kevin Hjortshøj O'Rourke |
| Policy Director | Charles Wyplosz |
| Chief Executive Officer | Tessa Ogden |

# About the Authors

**Laurence Ball** is a Professor of Economics at Johns Hopkins University, a Research Associate at the National Bureau of Economic Research, and a Visiting Scholar at the International Monetary Fund. He has previously visited a number of central banks, including the Federal Reserve, the Bank of Japan, the Bank of England, and the Reserve Bank of New Zealand. His research focuses on unemployment, inflation, and fiscal and monetary policy, and he is the author of *Money, Banking, and Financial Markets* (Worth Publishers, second edition 2012).

**Joseph E. Gagnon** is a senior fellow at the Peterson Institute for International Economics. Prior to September 2009, he was associate director in the Division of Monetary Affairs and the Division of International Finance at the US Federal Reserve Board. He has also served at the US Treasury Department and has taught at the Haas School of Business, University of California, Berkeley. He is author of *Flexible Exchange Rates for a Stable World Economy* (2011) and *The Global Outlook for Government Debt over the Next 25 years: Implications for the Economy and Public Policy* (2011). He has published numerous articles in economics journals, including the *Journal of International Economics*, the *Journal of Monetary Economics*, the *Review of International Economics*, and the *Journal of International Money and Finance*, and has contributed to several edited volumes. He received a BA from Harvard University in 1981 and a PhD in economics from Stanford University in 1987.

**Patrick Honohan** was Governor of the Central Bank of Ireland from 2009-2015, and has returned to Trinity College Dublin, where he was appointed Professor in 2007. He is a Research Fellow of CEPR and a Nonresident Senior Fellow at the Peterson Institute for International Economics. Previously he was a Senior Advisor in the World Bank working on issues of financial policy reform. During the 1980s he was Economic Advisor to the Taoiseach (Irish Prime Minister) and spent several years at the Economic and Social Research Institute, Dublin. A graduate of University College Dublin and of the London School of Economics, from which he received his PhD in 1978, Dr. Honohan has published widely on issues ranging from exchange rate regimes and purchasing-power parity, to migration, cost-benefit analysis and statistical methodology.

**Signe Krogstrup** is a Visiting Fellow at the Peterson Institute for International Economics. She previously served as Assistant Director and Deputy Head of Monetary Policy Analysis at the Swiss National Bank. In 2012–13, she served as an external expert on the Danish government appointed Committee on the Identification, Regulation, and Resolution of Systemically Important Financial Institutions in Denmark. She is a member of the World Economic Forum's Global Agenda Council (GAC) on Global Economic Imbalances (since 2014), and was on the GAC on the International Monetary System (2012–14). She has taught graduate courses in international macroeconomics and finance at the Graduate Institute in Geneva, University of St. Gallen, and at ETH in Zurich. Krogstrup received a doctoral degree in international economics from the Graduate Institute in 2003, and a master's degree in economics from the University of Copenhagen in 1999.

# Contents

*About the Authors* v
*Acknowledgements* ix
*List of conference participants* x
*Foreword* xvii

**Executive summary** xix

**1 Introduction and summary** 1

**2 The dangers of the lower bound** 5
2.1 A look at recent history 6
2.2 When will the constraint bind? A simple exercise 7
2.3 Dynamic simulations 9

**3 How to ease monetary policy when rates hit zero** 15
3.1 Negative interest rates 15
3.2 Quantitative easing 31
3.3 Helicopter money 44
3.4 Forward guidance 46
3.5 Beyond forward guidance: Committing to higher future inflation 47
3.6 Policy mix, interactions and financial stability 50

**4 Raising the inflation target** 53
4.1 Benefits of raising the inflation target 54
4.2 Costs of a higher inflation target 56
4.3 Credibility and the inflation target 59
4.4 How to implement a new target 60
4.5 What about a price level target? 61

**5 Monetary policy in a post-cash economy** 63
5.1 Markets are driving payments systems away from cash 64
5.2 Monetary policy without cash 66
5.3 Other policy aspects of post-cash economies 67

**6 Conclusions: So what should be done?** 71

## Discussions 73
The Geneva Report: Overview 73
Three questions 78
Lessons from the financial markets 88
Lessons from policymakers 93

## Appendix: The model used for simulations 101
*References* *103*

# Acknowledgements

We gratefully acknowledge comments and suggestions from Katrin Assenmacher, Tamim Bayoumi, Charles Bean, Olivier Blanchard, Bill Cline, Bill English, Jacob Kirkegaard, Don Kohn, Paolo Mauro, Athanasios Orphanides, Adam Posen, Glenn Rudebusch, Ted Truman, Angel Ubide, and Charles Wyplosz, and excellent research assistance by Sourav Dasgupta, Egor Gornostay and Owen Hauck. The views expressed in this report represent those of the authors, and not necessarily those of the institutions with which the authors are affiliated.

# List of conference participants

Ivan Adamovich
: Deputy CEO
Notenstein La Roche Private Bank Ltd
Zürich

Edmond Alphandery
: Chairman
Centre For European Policy Studies
Paris

Katrin Assenmacher
: Head of Monetary Policy Analysis
Swiss National Bank
Zürich

Richard Baldwin
: Professor of International Economics
The Graduate Institute, Geneva
Director, CEPR, London

Laurence Ball
: Professor of Economics
Johns Hopkins University

Vít Bárta
: Advisor to Governor
Czech National Bank
Prague

David Barwick
: Bureau Chief
MNI/Deutsche Boerse
Frankfurt

Agnès Benassy-Quere
: French Council of Economic Analysis
Professor, Paris School of Economics
University of Paris I

Mickael Benhaim
: Co-Head of Global Bonds, Fixed Income
Pictet Asset Management SA
Geneva

Jan Marc Berk
: Director
Economics and Research Division
De Nederlandsche Bank NV

Rémy Bersier
: Member of the Executive Board
Banque Julius Baer & Co. Ltd.
Geneva

| | |
|---|---|
| Robert Bichsel | Head of Banking System, Financial Stability<br>Swiss National Bank<br>Bern |
| Jean Boivin | Head of Economic and Markets Research<br>BlackRock Investment Institute<br>London |
| Claudio Borio | Head of Monetary and Economic Department<br>Bank for International Settlements (BIS)<br>Basel |
| Luigi Buttiglione | Head of Global Strategy<br>Brevan Howard Investment Products<br>Geneva |
| Per Callesen | Member of the Board of Governors<br>Danmarks National Bank |
| Nicolas Cuche-Curti | Head of Inflation Forecasting<br>Swiss National Bank |
| Jacques Delpla | Researcher<br>Toulouse School of Economics |
| Gene Frieda | Global Strategist<br>Moore Capital<br>London |
| Joseph Gagnon | Senior Fellow<br>Peterson Institute for International Economics<br>Washington, DC |
| Patrice Gautry | Chief Economist<br>Union Bancaire Privée (UBP)<br>Geneva |
| Gaston Gelos | Division Chief, Global Financial Stability Analysis<br>IMF<br>Washington, DC |
| Hans Genberg | Executive Director<br>The SEACEN Centre<br>Kuala Lumpur |
| Olivier Ginguene | CIO, Asset Allocation and Quantitative Investments<br>Pictet Asset Management<br>Geneva |

| | |
|---|---|
| Michel Girardin | Professor<br>University of Geneva |
| John Hassler | Professor of Economics<br>Institute for International Economic Studies<br>Stockholm University |
| Harald Hau | SFI Chaired Professor of Finance and Economics<br>University of Geneva<br>Geneva Finance Research Instittute |
| Patrick Honohan | Professor of Economics<br>Trinity College Dublin<br>Peterson Institute for International Economics<br>CEPR |
| Haizhou Huang | Managing Director and Member of Management Committee<br>China International Capital Corporation<br>Beijing |
| Yi Huang | Assistant Professor of Economics<br>Pictet Chair in Finance and Development<br>The Graduate Institute<br>Geneva |
| Thomas Jordan | Chairman of the Governing Board<br>Swiss National Bank<br>Zürich |
| Donald Kohn | Senior Fellow, Economic Studies<br>The Brookings Institution |
| Signe Krogstrup | Visiting Fellow<br>Peterson Institute for International Economics<br>Washington |
| Jean-Pierre Landau | Associate Professor of Economics<br>Sciences Po<br>Paris |
| Anne Le Lorier | Deputy Governor<br>Banque de France<br>Paris |
| Valérie Lemaigre | Chief Economist and Head of Investment Office<br>BCGE<br>Geneva |

| | |
|---|---|
| Carlos Lenz | Head of Economic Affairs<br>Swiss National Bank |
| Niels Lynggard Hansen | Director and Head of Economics<br>Danmarks Nationalbank |
| Andréa M. Maechler | Member of the Governing Board<br>Swiss National Bank |
| José Luis Malo de Molina | Counsellor for the Permanent Representation of Spain to the EU<br>Banco de España<br>Brussels |
| Thomas Mayer | Founding Director<br>Flossbach von Storch Research Institute |
| Carlo Monticelli | Vice-Governor<br>Council of Europe Development Bank<br>Paris |
| Thomas Moser | Alternate Member of the Governing Board<br>Swiss National Bank |
| Dierk Niepelt | Director<br>Study Center Gerzensee |
| Kiyohiko Nishimura | Professor, Faculty of Economics<br>The University of Tokyo |
| Ugo Panizza | Professor of International Economics<br>Pictet Chair in Finance and Development<br>The Graduate Institute<br>Geneva |
| Pierre Pâris | CEO<br>Banque Pâris Bertrand Sturdza<br>Geneva |
| Avinash Persaud | Chairman<br>Intelligence Capital Ltd<br>Non-resident senior fellow<br>Peterson Institute for International Economics |
| Adrien Pichoud | Economist<br>Global Macro and Fixed Income<br>Syz Asset Management<br>Geneva |

| | |
|---|---|
| Huw Pill | Chief European Economist<br>Goldman Sachs International |
| Renaud de Planta | Managing Partner<br>Pictet Group<br>Geneva |
| Kim-Andrée Potvin | Chief Operating Officer<br>BNP Paribas (Suisse) SA<br>Geneva |
| Jan Fredrik Qvigstad | Executive Director<br>General Staff<br>Central Bank of Norway |
| Gareth Ramsay | Director<br>Monetary Analysis<br>Bank of England |
| Jean-Christophe Reocreux | ALM Treasury Head<br>BNP Paribas (SUISSE) SA<br>Geneva |
| Märten Ross | Deputy Secretary General<br>Financial Policy and External Relations<br>Ministry of Finance of Estonia |
| Glenn Rudebusch | Director of Research<br>Economic Research<br>Federal Reserve Bank of San Francisco |
| Hans-Joerg Rudloff | Chairman<br>Marcuard Holding Ltd<br>London |
| Eric Santor | Chief<br>Canadian Economic Analysis<br>Bank of Canada |
| Ludger Schuknecht | Director General<br>Strategy and International Economy<br>German Federal Ministry of Finance |
| Torsten Slok | Chief International Economist<br>Managing Director<br>Deutsche Bank Securities<br>New York |

| | |
|---|---|
| Frank Smets | Adviser to the President<br>Counsel to the Executive Board<br>European Central Bank |
| Anthony Smouha | CEO<br>Atlanticomnium SA<br>Geneva |
| Jelena Stapf | Senior Economist<br>Head of G20 Presidency coordination team<br>Deutsche Bundesbank |
| Alexander Swoboda | Professor of Economics Emeritus<br>The Graduate Institute<br>Geneva |
| Leslie Teo | Chief Economist, Managing Director<br>Economics and Investment Strategy<br>GIC Private Limited<br>Singapore |
| Albi Tola | Senior Economist<br>International Monetary Relations<br>Swiss National Bank |
| Jan Toth | Deputy Governor<br>National Bank of Slovakia |
| Pascal Towbin | Economist, Financial Stability<br>Swiss National Bank |
| Edwin Truman | Senior Fellow<br>Peterson Institute for International Economics<br>Washington, DC |
| Sushil Wadhwani | CEO<br>Wadhwani Asset Management LLP<br>London |
| Sebastian Weber | Economist<br>European Central Bank |
| Xin Xiang Wen | Deputy Director General<br>Monetary Policy Department<br>The People's Bank of China |

Charles Wyplosz          Professor of International Economics
                         The Graduate Institute, Geneva
                         Director
                         ICMB
                         Geneva
                         Policy Director
                         CEPR
                         London

Attilio Zanetti          Head of Economic Analysis
                         Swiss National Bank

Tao Zhang                Deputy Governor
                         The People's Bank of China

Fritz Zurbruegg          Vice Chairman of the Governing Board
                         Department II
                         Swiss National Bank

# Foreword

The Geneva Reports on the World Economy are published annually by CEPR and ICMB and have been providing innovative analysis on important topical issues facing the global economy since 1999. This 18th report focuses on what central banks can do to stimulate economies when interest rates have reached zero. The authors argue that the negative interest rates and quantitative easing used by central banks in advanced economies since 2009 have been effective and that such policies could be expanded if needed.

To lessen future constraints on policy from the lower bound, the authors suggest that central banks consider adopting a modestly higher inflation target in the context of a periodic review of monetary policy objectives and operating procedures. They also propose options that could be adopted by policymakers to provide further stimulus in economies with underemployment and below-target inflation. First, they suggest that pushing interest rates further below zero can be done without adverse consequences. The authors argue that combining this with expanded quantitative easing, which has already been proven useful, is a means by which central banks can increase the level of stimulus. They also discuss the idea of a cashless economy, which would solve the lower bound problem by eliminating a riskless asset with zero nominal returns. This is not currently politically or practically realistic, but the authors would like to see it discussed as a future solution.

With most options having already been explored by central banks, the 18th Geneva Report aims at providing policymakers with a collection of stimulus tools that can be used to tackle the challenges of secular stagnation in modern advanced economies.

This report was produced following the 18th Geneva Conference on the World Economy held in May 2016. CEPR and the ICMB are very grateful to the authors and several discussants for their efforts in preparing material for this report, as well as to the conference attendees for their insightful comments. We are also thankful to Laurence Procter for her continued efficient organisation of the Geneva conference series, to Martina Hengge for recording and summarising the discussions, and to Simran Bola and Anil Shamdasani for their work in publishing the report. CEPR, which takes no institutional positions on economic policy matters, is delighted to provide a platform for an exchange of views on this topic.

Charles Wyplosz
Director, ICMB

Tessa Ogden
Chief Executive Officer, CEPR

September 2016

# Executive summary

Short-term interest rates have been near zero in advanced economies since 2009, making it difficult for central banks to cut rates further and provide needed economic stimulus. There is reason to believe that this lower bound problem will be common in the decades to come. This report asks (i) whether there is more that central banks can do to provide stimulus when rates are near zero; and (ii) whether policies exist that would lessen future constraints from the lower bound.

Many commentators give pessimistic answers to the first question, suggesting that central banks are 'out of ammunition' to stimulate the economy. We argue, to the contrary, that there is much that policymakers can and should do to provide further stimulus in environments with underemployment and inflation below target. We emphasise two policy options:

- *Negative interest rates.* Since 2014, some central banks have pushed nominal interest rates modestly below zero, providing some increase in stimulus. Although there is a limit to how far below zero interest rates can go, it is likely that rates could go somewhat further than what has been done so far without adverse consequences.

- *Quantitative easing.* Central banks, beginning with the Federal Reserve and the Bank of England, have already used this tool to mitigate the slumps in their economies since 2008. More stimulus can be provided if policymakers increase the scale of quantitative easing, and if they expand the range of assets they purchase to include risky assets such as equity.

Critics of quantitative easing and negative interest rates suggest that these policies have destabilising effects on banks and financial markets. We argue, however, that any side effects are manageable and not of a magnitude to justify timidity in using available tools to regain price stability and restore full employment.

Turning to the second question, policymakers should be more willing to adjust their monetary frameworks to loosen the constraint on traditional interest rate policy arising from the lower bound. The most obvious way to do so would be a modest increase in central banks' inflation targets, from the typical level of 2% to, say, 3% or 4%. Simulations of a simple macroeconomic model suggest that a higher inflation target would substantially reduce the frequency and severity of lower bound episodes, helping to avoid a future of chronic underemployment.

As with quantitative easing and negative interest rates, critics have raised objections to our proposed policy, but we argue these concerns are overblown. There is little reason to believe that modest increases in inflation targets would have major costs; in particular, such policy changes, properly managed, would not harm central bank credibility or cause an unmooring of inflation expectations. Indeed, central banks could gain credibility by demonstrating that they have the ability to adapt to changed circumstances in a deliberate and measured way.

Finally, the report examines a development that may eventually remove the lower bound on interest rates entirely: the trend towards cashless economies. If cash ceases to exist, so there is no riskless asset with a zero nominal return, central banks can make nominal interest rates as negative as needed to spur recoveries from recessions. As payments technologies evolve, some countries are already well on their way to eliminating the use of cash. An abrupt abolition of cash and an immediate move to deeply negative interest rates is not practically or politically realistic, but some day we may live in cashless economies in which memories of the lower bound problem are dim.

# 1 Introduction and summary

The global financial crisis of 2008-09 ushered in the worst recession in advanced economies since the 1930s. Central banks initially responded by reducing policy interest rates sharply. Soon these rates approached zero, raising the spectre of a liquidity trap – the point at which further conventional monetary expansion becomes impossible. In an effort to provide further stimulus, central banks experimented with a range of unconventional policies, including guidance on the future stance of policy, extensive outright asset purchases (quantitative easing, or QE), and exchange rate management. Negative interest rates were brought into the mix later, as some central banks probed just how low their policy rates could safely and effectively go.

Unconventional expansionary monetary policies have been effective in easing financial conditions, producing a greater recovery of output and employment than would otherwise have occurred. Nonetheless, policy action taken since the crisis was not strong enough or fast enough to avoid a disappointing macroeconomic performance. Recovery has been slow compared to recoveries from past deep recessions; eight years after the crisis, much of the world is still far from full employment. In the Eurozone, for example, where the unemployment rate jumped from about 7% in 2008 to over 12% in 2013, the rate is still 10% today. Furthermore, Eurozone inflation has undershot even its low target for three years now and has been stuck at around zero since 2014.

The two main questions addressed in this report are: "Do central banks have effective tools for economic stimulus when nominal interest rates reach zero?" and "How can central banks reduce the likelihood of hitting the lower bound in the future?" We conclude that, even when nominal interest rates have fallen to zero, there is more that central banks can do to stimulate economic growth and inflation. Furthermore, there are policy options available that could reduce the likelihood of hitting zero again in the future.

We begin in Section 2 by characterising the challenges posed by the lower bound – both the damage arising from the lower bound on nominal interest rates since 2008, and dangers for the future. A simple macroeconomic model (calibrated to the US experience, but the Eurozone would have qualitatively similar features) suggests that annual unemployment rates averaged more than 1 percentage point higher from 2009 through 2015, compared to a hypothetical scenario with no constraint on the Federal Reserve's ability to lower interest rates. Excess unemployment would have been even higher if the Fed had not used forward guidance and QE.

Looking to the future, if zero is considered a lower bound on nominal rates, this constraint on policy is likely to bind whenever unemployment is little more than a percentage point above its long-run level – that is, in mild as well as severe recessions. This reflects the low level to which the neutral real interest rate has trended and the low inflation targets of central banks, which together imply that nominal interest rates will be chronically low and central banks' ability to reduce rates in downturns will be sharply limited.

Yet the lower bound on interest rates does not render central banks helpless, either today or in the future. In Section 3, we review the scope for central bank action to promote economic recovery when rates hit zero. We focus on negative policy interest rates, QE and communication about future policies. Exchange rate policy could also be part of the policy mix in some particular circumstances, but we do not discuss it.

First, it is possible to move nominal short-term policy rates into negative territory, thereby loosening monetary policy further through standard means. Several central banks have pushed policy rates below zero, and these negative rates have transmitted to domestic asset prices and the exchange rate in much the same way as cuts in policy rates have done when they were still positive. Moreover, concerns about the impact of negative policy rates on the functioning of the banking system have not been validated in practice to date. It seems likely that rates can be pushed even lower than has been attempted so far, at least by a modest amount, without unduly adverse side effects.

Second, central banks have a range of options for easing through QE. These programmes have already had substantial effects in the countries that implemented them. In the United States, for example, it is estimated that QE purchases of long-term bonds between 2008 and 2015 had macroeconomic effects equivalent to those of a sustained reduction of about 200 to 250 basis points in the policy rate. With a greater volume of purchases, the effects could have been almost proportionately greater. Another approach adopted by some central banks is subsidised and targeted lending to the banking system.

QE could be expanded further by widening the range of assets that central banks purchase to include risky assets such as corporate debt and equities. For given quantities of asset purchases, this broader version of QE could well have stronger effects on asset prices and costs of funds, and hence on economic activity, than purchases of government bonds.

Potential side effects of expansionary monetary policy have been stressed by some commentators. These include the risk of an overshoot resulting in a surge of inflation, the danger of asset price bubbles, disintermediation of the banking system (and hoarding of cash), challenges to the profitability of banks and/or the central bank, the potential for loss of monetary policy independence and perceived distributional impacts. There is so far little evidence of significant adverse side effects. In general, such risks are lower in the depressed conditions that normally accompany a liquidity trap; should they occur, the most important side effects can be mitigated or managed.

Of course, monetary policy cannot solve all economic problems; in particular, it cannot raise an economy's potential rate of growth. But monetary policy can deliver any desired rate of inflation over the medium term and it can help to stabilise output around potential. Fiscal policy may be useful in speeding recovery from a deep recession and reducing the burden on monetary policy. Because we focus on what central banks can do, fiscal policy is beyond the scope of this report. However, we do discuss briefly the combined fiscal and monetary policy known as 'helicopter money'.

Although policymakers have tools for stimulus at the lower bound, full employment would be more secure if policy frameworks were adjusted to reduce or eliminate the likelihood that nominal rates hit zero. The most obvious of such adjustments would be a modest increase in central banks' inflation targets, which we discuss in Section 4. Low levels of nominal interest rates result both from

lower real interest rates, and from the low inflation targets of advanced-economy central banks – typically 2% or lower. Raising the target to, say, 3% or 4% would make a worthwhile reduction in the frequency with which the economy hits the zero bound and the resulting risk of chronic underemployment.

The apparent secular decline of the equilibrium real rate of interest and the severity of the Great Recession have moved the cost-benefit calculation in favour of a higher inflation target. While there are non-trivial issues of tactics (which we discuss) in managing a transition to a higher inflation target, fears of an unmooring of inflation expectations or damage to central bank credibility are overblown. Indeed, central banks likely would gain credibility by demonstrating that they have the ability to adapt to changed circumstances in a deliberate and measured way.

Section 5 reviews what may eventually remove the lower bound on nominal interest rates, namely, the trend towards a cashless society. The existence of cash (i.e. currency notes) – an asset provided by the central bank and that guarantees a nominal return of zero – is the underlying reason for the lower bound. If cash did not exist, there would be no lower bound, and policymakers facing an economic downturn could make rates as negative as needed to spur a strong and rapid recovery.

Cash is steadily being replaced by new electronic means of payments in retail transactions. This trend is likely to gain pace, driven by market forces, and eventually cash will become redundant in most countries. Some countries are already well on the way. An abrupt abolition of cash in order to facilitate an immediate move to deeply negative interest rates is clearly both politically and practically unrealistic. Yet, someday, the existence of cash may be remembered in the same way as the gold standard – an obsolete payments technology whose persistence hampered economic performance

# 2 The dangers of the lower bound

During the Great Depression of the 1930s, Keynes (1936, Chapter 17) pointed out that monetary policy could become impotent in a "liquidity trap" if interest rates reached a lower bound.[1] For half a century afterwards, this point was largely a theoretical curiosity, a topic for trick questions on economics exams. It was not relevant to practical monetary policy because interest rates were usually well above zero, even during recessions, and policymakers had no trouble reducing rates to stimulate the economy when they wanted to do so.

Table 2.1 shows, however, that since the mid-1990s, and in contrast to early decades, policy rates have spent quite some time at or close to zero in advanced economies, sharply constraining central banks' ability to respond to economic downturns. This problem has arisen partly because central banks have targeted low levels of inflation, which generally imply low nominal interest rates. In addition, the long-run level of real interest rates has fallen.[2]

The remainder of this section reviews recent history and presents simulations of a simple macroeconomic model to judge the costs of the zero bound in recent years and to shed light on the risks for the future.

**Table 2.1** Yearly average policy rates in selected advanced economies

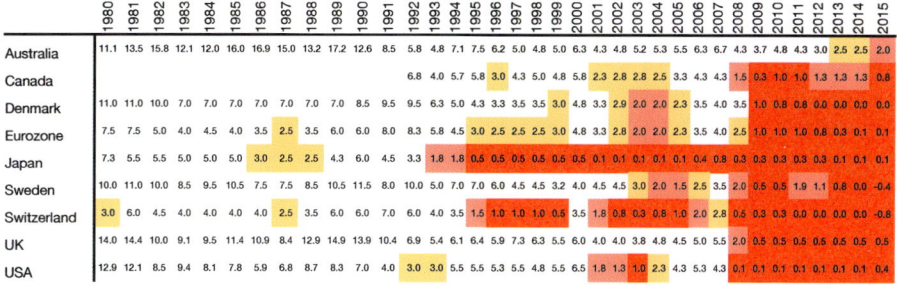

*Notes:* Red cells are years with policy rates at or below 1%. Light red cells are years where policy rates are at or below 2%, and light yellow cells are years with policy rates below 3%.

*Sources:* IMF International Financial Statistics and Swiss National Bank.

---

1  Although Keynes originally introduced the term "liquidity trap" in a narrower context focusing on long-term interest rates, we will use the term to describe any situation where monetary policy is constrained by a lower bound on policy interest rates.
2  This point is emphasised in much recent research, including the 17th Geneva Report on the Word Economy (Bean et al., 2015).

## 2.1 A look at recent history

In the 1970s and early 1980s, accommodative monetary policy in response to the two oil price surges resulted in inflation reaching double-digit levels in many advanced economies, prompting vigorous policy reaction. US President Gerald Ford declared inflation "public enemy number one" in 1974; in 1980, British Prime Minister Margaret Thatcher stated: "I tell you that inflation is the biggest destroyer of all – of industry, of jobs, of savings, and of society"; and French President Francois Mitterrand spoke in 1983 of a battle to "stop the infernal machine" of inflation. Elsewhere in Europe, markedly differing inflation rates gave rise to the volatile exchange rate movements that were an important driver of the creation of the euro. Vigorous efforts to control inflation, such as those of Paul Volcker in the United States and of the Thatcher government in the United Kingdom, meant that inflation in advanced economies had largely come under control by the late 1980s. In the 1990s and early 2000s, many countries began targeting an inflation rate around 2%, either explicitly or implicitly, and achieving that target.

Yet this "conquest" of inflation (Sargent, 1999), combined with an apparent secular trend decline in real interest rates, has had a side-effect that policymakers did not anticipate: the emergence of the lower bound on interest rates as an important constraint hampering macroeconomic stabilisation measures.

The key distinction between nominal and real interest rates is summarised in the Fisher equation, defining the real interest rate as the difference between the nominal interest rate and expected inflation:

$$r = i - \pi^e. \tag{2.1}$$

As inflation rates settled at low levels, so did expected inflation and nominal interest rates. As long as physical currency has a fixed yield of zero, it is difficult for central banks to push rates of return on other assets too far below zero; investors will sell those assets to hold cash, which is safe and liquid. If the normal level of the nominal interest rate is low, that limits the scope for cutting rates in a downturn. For most of the period since World War II, central banks have used interest rate cuts as their primary tool for expansionary countercyclical policy, and sharp rate cuts have been critical to strong recoveries from recessions. Losing the capacity to cut interest rates creates the risk that future recessions could be protracted.

Once central banks started targeting inflation rates around 2% in the 1990s, it did not take long for the zero bound to emerge as a problem. The Japanese financial crisis and economic slump of the 1990s led the Bank of Japan to reduce its policy rate to 0.1% in 1999, yet output remained depressed and Japanese policy interest rates have been 0.5% or less ever since. The US recession of 2001, which was one of the mildest since World War II, led to a peak unemployment rate of only 6.3%. In this episode, the United States did not hit the lower bound, but it came close, with the federal funds rate reaching 1%. The Eurozone avoided outright recession in 2001-3, but the ECB nevertheless lowered its main repo rate to 2%, and its deposit rate to 1%.

Then, only five years later, the financial crisis and Great Recession of 2008 struck the United States and spread around the world. By early 2009, interest rates in most advanced economies were near zero. The US federal funds rate was lowered to less than 0.25%, where it stayed for seven years. Money market rates in the Eurozone fell in 2009 to the level of 0.25%, to which the ECB lowered its deposit rate. Following a brief recovery, a further recession in the Eurozone in 2011-12 saw interest rates reduced again, eventually this time to below zero.

At the March 2009 meeting of the Federal Reserve's monetary policy committee, Janet Yellen (then president of the Federal Reserve Bank of San Francisco) stated that "optimal policy simulations would take the fed funds rate to negative 6%".[3] Since then, the presence of a lower bound has limited the ability of conventional expansionary interest rate policy. During the Great Recession, central banks have had to resort to other measures, some of which were designed as much to respond to impaired money market functioning as to increase aggregate demand.

If a mild recession pushed the desired interest rate to +1% and a severe recession pushed it to −6% in the 2000s, these economies are likely to hit the zero bound in a typical recession. The same is clearly true in Japan, where policy rates have been below 1% for more than 20 years.

The risk posed by the zero bound is exacerbated by the apparent downward trend in the normal or neutral level of the short-term real interest rate—that is to say, the rate at which aggregate demand and the potential level of output are equated without inflationary or deflationary pressure. The downward trend in risk-free rates over recent years has convinced many researchers that the neutral short-term rate in most advanced economies has fallen by a percentage point or more since the early 2000s – perhaps from 2%, the level famously assumed by Taylor (1993), to 1% or even lower (Laubach and Williams, 2015). Clearly, such a reduction increases the frequency with which the lower bound will be reached by central banks addressing a downturn.

## 2.2 When will the constraint bind? A simple exercise

We can get a feel for how frequently short-term policy interest rates are likely to hit zero by examining simple versions of two macroeconomic relationships: the Taylor Rule, which captures how many central banks adjust interest rates; and the Phillips curve, which captures the short-run interactions of unemployment and inflation.

A simple Taylor rule equation such as (2.2) below provides a good approximation to actual central banking policy in the Great Moderation period of 1987-2007.[4]

$$i = r^* + \pi + 0.5(\pi - \pi^*) - 2.0u, \qquad (2.2)$$

---

[3] The transcript is available at www.federalreserve.gov/monetarypolicy/fomchistorical2009.htm. Other versions of policy rules yielded numbers in the range of −5% or so (Rudebusch, 2009).
[4] See Rudebusch (2009) for the United States, and Blattner and Margaritov (2010) for the Eurozone.

where $r^*$ is the neutral real interest rate, $\pi^*$ is the inflation target, and $u$ is the deviation of unemployment from its natural rate. According to this equation, when inflation is at its target and unemployment is at the natural rate, the central bank sets its policy rate $i$ equal to $r^* + \pi$, implying that the real rate equals the neutral rate $r^*$. The nominal policy rate rises by 1.5 percentage points for each 1 point rise in the inflation rate and by two points for each percentage point fall in the unemployment rate.[5]

Recent research on the Phillips curve for both the United States and Europe suggests that, if inflation expectations are anchored at the central bank's target, a 1 percentage point rise in the rate of unemployment reduces inflation by about 0.5 percentage points (Ball, 2015; Blanchard, 2016):

$$\pi = \pi^* - 0.5u. \tag{2.3}$$

Substituting this simple Phillips curve into the Taylor rule allows us to derive the interest rate as a function of the unemployment rate:

$$i = r^* + \pi^* - 2.75u. \tag{2.4}$$

Here, the coefficient of 2.75 on unemployment reflects both the direct effect of unemployment on the interest rate in the Taylor rule and the fact that higher unemployment reduces inflation, which further reduces the interest rate in the rule.

We can use this last equation to determine how high the unemployment rate must rise for the zero bound on interest rates to constrain policy; that is to say, to prevent the central bank from following its usual Taylor rule. That occurs if the right side of equation (2.4) is less than zero, which is the case if the unemployment gap $u$ is greater than $(r^* + \pi^*)/2.75$. We will use the symbol $\hat{u}$ for this critical level of unemployment.

In most advanced economies, the inflation target $\pi^*$ is close to 2%. If, as we have discussed, the neutral real rate $r^*$ is as low as 1%, our formula yields $\hat{u} = 1.1$. In words, if a recession pushes the unemployment rate more than 1.1 percentage points above the natural rate, the zero bound will prevent the countercyclical interest rate policy response that was normal during the Great Moderation period.

An unemployment gap of 1.1 percentage points would arise after a very mild economic downturn. Using estimates of the natural rate of unemployment from the Congressional Budget Office (CBO), for the eight US recessions since 1960, the peak in the gap following the recession exceeded 1.1 points in seven cases (all but the 1970 recession), and in those cases the peak unemployment gap averaged 2.7 points. The gap reached 1.3 percentage points following the mild recession of 2001.[6] Therefore, if future recessions are similar in magnitude to recessions of the last half century, they will cause interest rates to hit zero far more often than not.

---

5   A coefficient of −2 on unemployment is equivalent to a coefficient of 1 on the output gap, assuming an Okun's Law relationship in which a 1 point drop in unemployment corresponds to a 2 point rise in output.
6   The Eurozone's history is shorter, its labour market more fragmented, and measures of the Eurozone-wide unemployment gap much debated, but the double-dip Great Recession pushed Eurozone unemployment up almost 5 percentage points from 2008 to 2013.

If recessions continue to occur with their frequency in the United States since 1960 – about once every seven years on average – the economy will spend a lot of time at the zero bound.[7]

## 2.3 Dynamic simulations

To illustrate the potential scale of economic damage caused by the zero bound on interest rates, we perform simulations of a simple macroeconomic model, consisting of three equations. The first is a policy rule: we assume the interest rate is determined by the Taylor rule (equation (2.2)) when that rule implies a non-negative rate, and zero when the Taylor rule implies a negative rate. The second equation is a small variation on the Phillips curve above (equation (2.3)) capturing dynamics that are more realistic: the inflation rate in a quarter depends on unemployment gaps in the previous four quarters. The third equation is a dynamic IS equation based on the work of Rudebusch and Svensson (1999) and Laubach and Williams (2000). It expresses the level of unemployment as a function of past levels of unemployment and of the real interest rate. An error term in this equation captures shocks to aggregate spending, such as the decreases in consumption and investment resulting from the 2008 financial crisis.

The Appendix to this report describes the model in more detail. Here, we present simulations of the model (calibrated on the US economy) that address two questions: (i) How much did the zero bound exacerbate the high unemployment of the Great Recession?; and (ii) How much is the zero bound likely to constrain policy and raise unemployment in future recessions?

### 2.3.1 Revisiting the Great Recession

Figure 2.1 presents two paths for the central bank policy rate (the federal funds rate in this US calibration), the unemployment rate, and the inflation rate from 2008 through 2015. One of the cases in the figure is the actual historical data for these variables in the US. The other is a counterfactual simulation, beginning in 2009:Q1 (the first quarter after the federal funds rate reached a target range of 0 to 0.25%), of what would have happened if there were no zero bound on interest rates. In this simulation, the federal funds rate is always set by the Taylor rule, even when that implies a negative rate. We assume the same Phillips and IS equations in the two cases, and also the same shocks to these two equations, which we construct by taking the differences between actual inflation and unemployment and the fitted values from our equations (see the Appendix for details on our computations). Note that the Fed did conduct QE during this period, so the historical data do not reflect a pure lower bound outcome. We explore the impact of QE separately in a simulation in Section 3, where we show that unemployment would have been higher, and inflation lower, if the Fed had not done any QE at the zero bound.

---

[7] The CBO series for the natural rate is available in the FRED database at the Federal Reserve Bank of St. Louis. Our finding of a low value for $\hat{u}$, the unemployment gap needed for interest rates to hit zero, is robust. For example, if we were to assume $r^*$ is 2 rather than 1, $\hat{u}$ would rise from 1.1 only to 1.5, still considerably smaller than the unemployment gap in a typical recession. If we were to reduce the coefficient on unemployment in the Phillips curve from 0.5 to 0.25, implying a smaller reduction of inflation in a downturn, $\hat{u}$ would rise from 1.1 to 1.3.

**Figure 2.1** The Great Recession with and without the zero lower bound

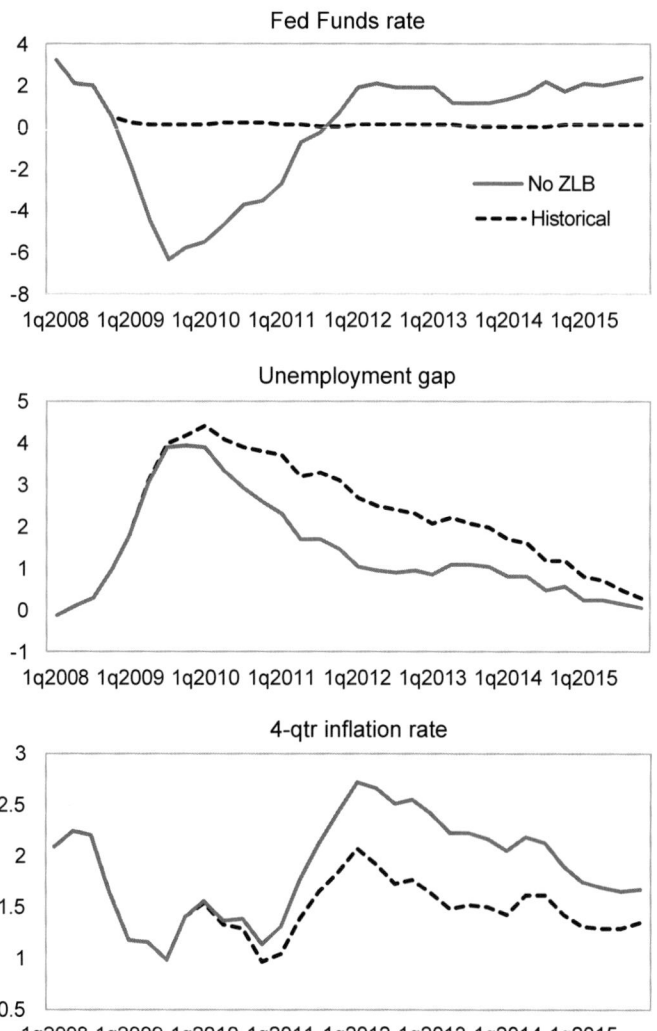

In actual history, the federal funds rate was close to zero for the 28 quarters from the beginning of 2009 to the end of 2015. In our no-lower-bound counterfactual, by contrast, the federal funds rate falls to about –6% in early 2009, essentially equal to Yellen's estimate of the optimal policy rate in March 2009 (discussed above in Section 2.1).[8] Because of the large cut in interest rates, the unemployment rate, after spiking up in early 2009, falls more rapidly in the simulation than it did in actual history. By 2012, the unemployment gap is about 1 percentage point in the counterfactual, while it is still greater than 2 percentage points in the

---

8   As discussed in Section 3.2 below, the QE adopted by the Fed in 2009-10 was equivalent to a cut in the policy rate of 1 percentage point. Adjusted for the effects of QE, Yellen's optimal policy rate would have been –5%.

historical data. By Okun's Law, a 1 percentage point reduction in unemployment implies a gain of 2 percentage points of output. The cumulative reduction in unemployment from 2009 through 2015 implies a cumulative gain in output equal to 14% of annual output.[9]

In the counterfactual case, a faster recovery means that monetary conditions can normalise more quickly. We see in the figure that the federal funds rate becomes positive in 2011, more than four years before the Fed actually increased the rate. We also see that the faster recovery raises inflation, which is close to its 2% target from 2011 through 2015 in the counterfactual.

In 2009, it would not have been feasible for the Fed to reduce interest rates to –6%. Through the rest of the report, we present alternative simulations based on this model to support the discussion of tools and targets. In discussing negative interest rates in Section 3, we simulate another counterfactual where the Fed would have pushed rates *somewhat* below zero, but by less than implied by the Taylor Rule. We also simulate the degree to which QE helped to prevent an even worse outcome, and by implication, the degree to which additional QE could have substituted for further rate cuts. In our discussion of raising the inflation target in Section 4, we examine what might have happened if the economy entered the Great Recession with a higher inflation target and higher nominal interest rates, so that greater conventional easing was feasible despite the lower bound on nominal rates.

In at least one respect, our estimates of the damage from the lower bound constraint are conservative because they ignore the possibility that deep recessions can have long-lasting, or even permanent, effects on employment and output not modelled here. A number of studies find considerable evidence of such 'hysteresis' effects (Ball, 2014; Blanchard et al., 2015). By reducing the depth and length of the recession, aggressive monetary easing may reduce these hysteresis effects and thus yield benefits that are greater than those captured in our simple model.

### 2.3.1 What the future might hold

How often will the lower bound constrain policy in the future, and what will the economic damage be? As Williams (2014) emphasises, the answer depends on the sizes of shocks to the economy, which determine how much central banks need to adjust interest rates to offset the shocks. It is difficult to know whether the underlying sources of economic volatility will be more or less severe in the future than they have been in various parts of history, and we will not take a stand on that issue. Moreover, the economic damage from episodes at the zero bound depends critically on the ability of central banks to use unconventional policy, which we discuss in Section 3. Therefore, we will not make predictions of the effects of the zero bound on future unemployment fluctuations or on economic welfare. However, as we have already discussed, there is good reason to believe that conventional monetary policy will be constrained by the lower bound even in modest economic downturns.

---

9   Chung et al. (2011) analyse the effects of the zero bound from 2008 through 2011 using a large macroeconomic model – the Fed's FRB/US model. Despite some quantitative differences, their overall conclusion has the same spirit as ours: "the severity of the ZLB [zero lower bound] constraint has been considerable over the past few years".

Here we illustrate the possible costs of the lower bound constraint with two sets of simulations, the results of which are shown in Figure 2.2. In each simulation, the economy starts in a steady state with inflation at its 2% target, the real interest rate at its neutral level of 1% and hence the nominal rate at 3%, and the unemployment gap at zero. We assume the economy is hit by a series of shocks to the IS equation over six quarters. In the first set of simulations (the upper panels), the shocks are half the size of the IS shocks that occurred during the Great Recession from 2008Q4 through 2010Q1.[10] We simulate the model first imposing a zero lower bound on the fed funds rate (the solid line) and then relaxing that restriction (the dashed line), so that the funds rate can be as negative as implied by the Taylor rule (no zero lower bound). In the zero lower bound simulation, the fed funds rate is stuck at zero for eight quarters. In the unrestricted simulation, the fed funds rate bottoms out around −1.5% and the unemployment gap is noticeably smaller, especially after about ten quarters.

By historical standards, this is a significant but not large recession – the peak unemployment gap is somewhat larger than the one in the recession of the early 2000s, about the same as in the recession of the early 1990s, and significantly less than the average for the eight recessions since 1960.

When a shock pushes the interest rate to zero, that harms the economy by slowing recovery from the shock. It also puts the economy in a fragile position. History teaches us that recessionary shocks can occur at any time, and sometimes one shock follows quickly after another. If a new shock occurs and the economy is already at the lower bound, the central bank has no interest rate ammunition to use to counter the new shock, and its effects can be greatly amplified as a result.

The second set of simulations shows the potential cost of the zero lower bound if the economy is hit with two modest recessions two years apart. The lower panels in Figure 2.2 display the cumulative unemployment gap when a sequence of IS shocks half as large as those of the Great Recession is repeated eight quarters later. The zero lower bound binds for 21 quarters and it binds by a larger amount; the unrestricted Taylor rule would have the interest rate at −3%. The damage caused by two modest recessions in terms of the unemployment gap is far greater than twice the damage of one modest recession. This nonlinearity between the magnitude of the shocks and the magnitude of the damage reflects the nonlinearity of the policy rule when the zero lower bound is enforced.

---

10  Unlike the previous simulation, this simulation is not limited to the period in which the federal funds rate was near zero. This allows us to include the effect of the demand shock in 2008Q4.

**Figure 2.2** A half Great Recession (upper) and two half Great Recessions (lower)

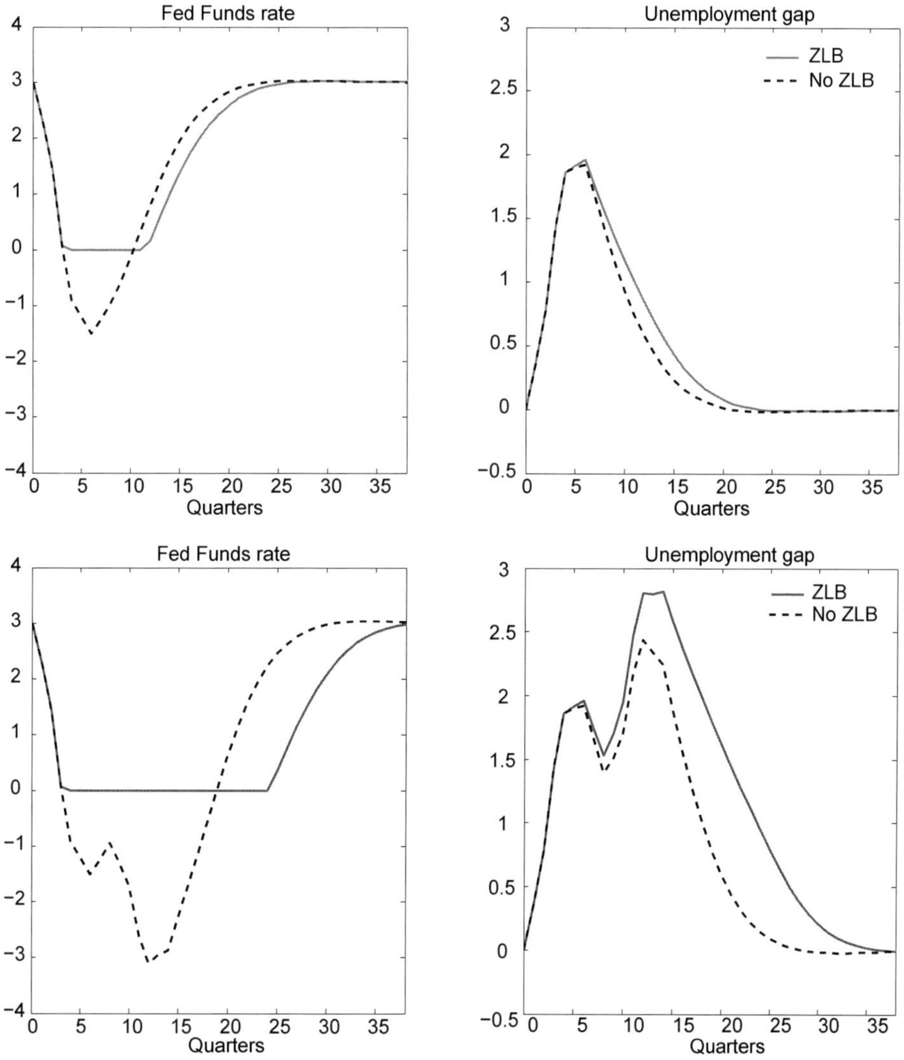

# 3 How to ease monetary policy when rates hit zero

Even when nominal short-term interest rates have reached zero, central banks do not lack tools for further stimulating the economy. In this section, we discuss negative interest rates and QE, which have both been used with some success in recent years. We also briefly consider how communication about future policy intentions can be used to influence inflation expectations, and hence real interest rates. We argue that there is considerable potential for using these more aggressively. We make the case for the benefits of these policies and discuss concerns that have been raised about potential adverse side effects.

## 3.1 Negative interest rates

The primary obstacle constituting a lower bound on interest rates is the availability of zero-interest-paying physical currency, or cash. As interest rates fall further below zero, there is some point at which households, firms and banks will choose to hold cash rather than assets that pay negative rates. The lower bound on policy rates was long considered to be zero.

Beginning in 2012, a few central banks have pushed key policy interest rates below zero for the first time.[11] Holdings of cash have not increased. Technical and legal issues relating to negative interest rates have proved to be surmountable, but there remain challenges for the business model of retail banking and money market mutual funds.

### 3.1.1 Recent experiences

Danmarks Nationalbank, the ECB, the Swiss National Bank (SNB), Sweden's Riksbank and the Bank of Japan have reduced their monetary policy rates into negative territory in the past years (Figure 3.1).[12] These unprecedented moves have illustrated that policy rates can turn negative without setting off an immediate scramble into cash or impairing the functioning of key financial sector firms. They have also showed that movements of policy rates into negative territory do transmit to money and capital markets largely through the usual channels.

---

11 The Riksbank lowered the interest rate on its deposit facility below zero as far back as 2009, but this is not a key rate in Swedish money markets and does not transmit to market rates.
12 In March 2016, Magyar Nemzeti Bank, the Hungarian central bank, lowered the rate on its deposit facility to -5 basis points.

16  *What Else Can Central Banks Do?*

**Figure 3.1**  Monetary policy interest rates in negative interest rate countries

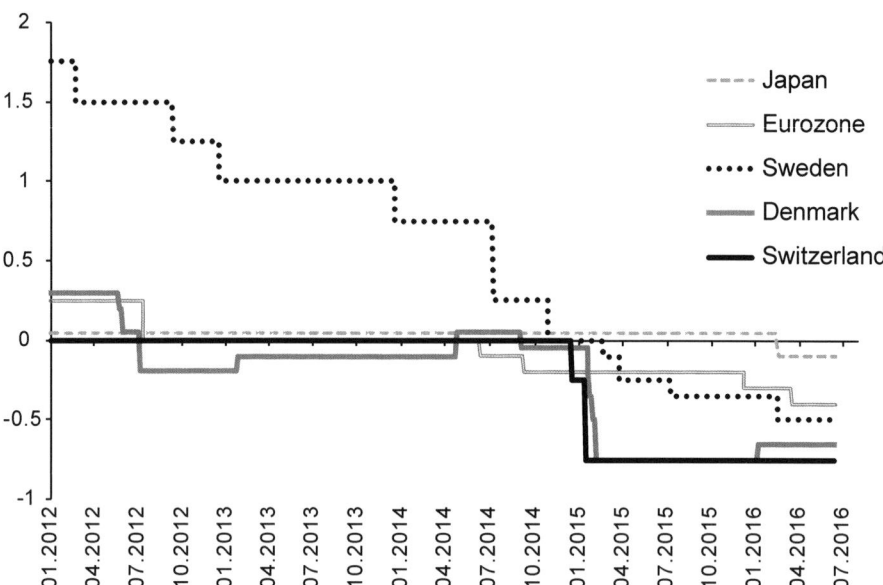

The Riksbank has set the most deeply negative policy rate, –125 basis points for overnight deposits, but few deposits are made at this rate because Swedish banks normally place any excess liquidity in one-week reverse repos (which currently yield –50 basis points). In terms of rates that do affect banks and hence transmit to money markets, Danmarks Nationalbank and the SNB have gone furthest into negative territory, at –75 basis points for overnight deposits.[13] The ECB deposit rate was reduced in several steps, reaching –40 basis points in March 2016.

Implementation of negative central bank deposit rates has differed across countries (Bech and Malkhozov 2016). Danmarks Nationalbank, the SNB, and the Bank of Japan have exempted substantial parts of their deposits from negative rates through tiering systems. The exempted tiers reduce the overall impact of the negative interest rate on banks' interest income, while the negative rate still applies to additional deposits made by the banks in the central bank deposit facility. This means that the negative rate applies to the marginal money market operation, and hence that it transmits more broadly to money markets. The ECB and the Riksbank have not adopted tiered systems.

---

13  The Swiss policy rate is expected to remain at this level or to go even lower for the coming two-to-three years. Danmarks Nationalbank reversed course in January 2016 and lifted the policy rate –65 basis points; markets expect Danish rates to rise gradually.

### 3.1.2 Transmission

The experience so far is that policy rate cuts into negative territory transmit through largely the same transmission channels as cuts in positive territory. Exceptions relate chiefly to retail bank deposit and lending interest rates, to which transmission has often been more sluggish and has varied substantially across countries.

*Transmission to bond and money markets*

Figures 3.2 to 3.6 show that in all five countries, short-term money market interest rates have responded quickly to the implementation of negative policy rates. In Denmark, the money market rate – which has a longer maturity than the policy rate – has moved higher than the policy rate, but this reflects expectations of an imminent rise in the policy rate, not a lack of transmission.

**Figure 3.2** Denmark: Policy rate, money and capital market interest rates

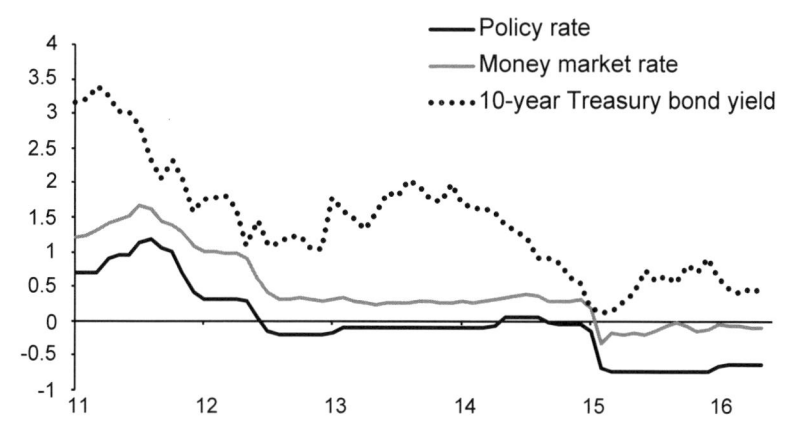

*Source:* Haver Analytics.

To the extent that market participants assume the existence of some lower bound to policy rates, it is natural for long-term yields (reflecting, among other things, expectations of future short-term rates) to respond less to reductions in policy rates below zero than they would when rates are positive (Ruge-Murcia, 2006).[14] On the other hand, current ongoing research suggests that rate cuts below zero can lower the market's perception of the effective lower bound, thereby widening the expected future distribution of interest rates into negative territory, and thereby lowering long-term yields (Grisse et al., 2016, Lemke et al., 2016). Reductions of policy rates into negative territory have generally been associated with reductions along the rest of the yield curve (Figures 3.2 to 3.6). In some countries, the yield on government bonds has dipped below zero for maturities as long as ten years. In Japan, the long-term yield fell by as much as the policy rate in the hours after the January 2016 announcement, and has declined further

---

[14] This effect has been found to be empirically relevant (Swanson and Williams, 2014a, 2014b; Grisse 2015).

since.[15] In Denmark and Sweden, long-term yields have increased more recently, reflecting expectations that growth and inflation are picking up, and hence that policy rate rises will be forthcoming. Corporate yields have occasionally turned negative; Figures 3.3 and 3.6 illustrate this for the Eurozone and Switzerland, respectively. In Japan, the negative rate introduced in early 2016 transmitted only partially into corporate yields, implying higher risk premiums.

**Figure 3.3**  Eurozone: Policy rate, money and capital market interest rates

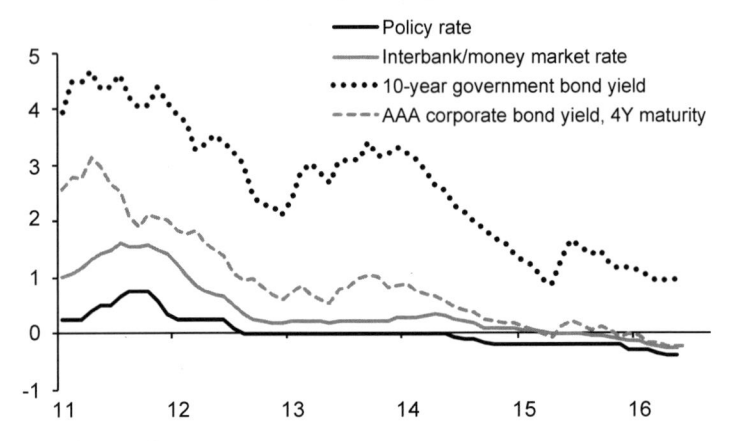

*Sources:* Haver Analytics and Datastream.

**Figure 3.4**  Japan: Policy rate, money and capital market interest rates

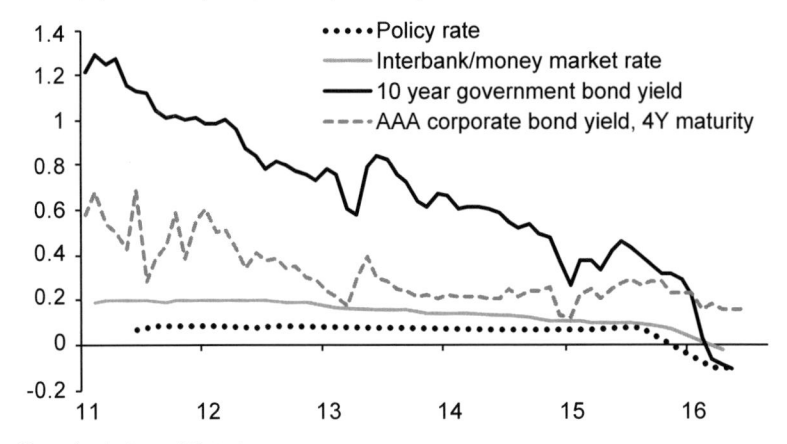

*Sources:* Haver Analytics and Datastream.

---

15  The strong drop in the long-term yield suggests that the cut succeeded in loosening the perceived lower bound constraint on interest rates, and hence lowered the future distribution of policy rates. The long-term yield continued to drop even further in the following days, but this may also reflect an increase in risk aversion and flight to safety that later ensued.

**Figure 3.5** Sweden: policy rate, money and capital market rates and bank interest rates

*Source:* Haver Analytics.

**Figure 3.6** Switzerland: Policy rate, money and capital market interest rates.

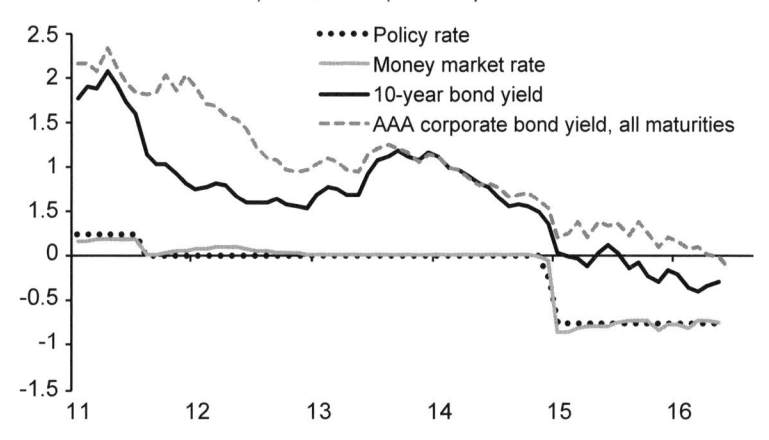

*Sources:* Haver Analytics and Datastream.

*Transmission to bank interest rates*

The transmission of rate cuts to bank interest rates has been sluggish, as a resistance of bank deposit rates to go below zero has been evident.[16] This resistance is not universal. Indeed, banks are charging negative rates to some corporate and institutional investor deposits in some countries (Shin, 2016). Average deposit

---
16 There is a question as to the legality of negative rates on bank deposits in Japan. Although not a conclusive ruling, the Financial Law Board of Japan has opined that "it would not be possible for a bank ... to set its posted rates applicable to deposits ... at a negative rate" (www.flb.gr.jp, 16 February 2016).

rates for non-financial firms in Denmark, for example, are slightly negative, and bank deposit rates for pension and insurance funds have turned more negative (Danmarks Nationalbank 2016). In Switzerland, large time deposit rates have turned negative.

However, there is little evidence so far that banks are passing negative interest rates through to their retail depositors.[17] Insured retail deposits are an attractive source of financing for a bank in normal times, and a retail customer can often be cross-sold many other value-added banking products. Banks are reluctant to lose market share for insured deposits, which they may not easily regain when interest rates turn positive. Moving to a negative interest rate could be a salient event that would cause retail customers to 'shop around'. Given the inertia normally characterising retail bank relationships, the bank that makes the first move into negative deposit rates for retail customers could experience a hard-to-reverse loss of market share. Besides, charging interest on retail deposits would be likely to have a negative impact on the wider public image of banks that begin to do so.[18] Moreover, banks may fear that retail customers are more likely to switch from deposits to cash as the interest rate on deposits falls below the zero rate on cash. We discuss the issue of migration out of electronic money into cash further below. Finally, transmission to deposit rates may simply take time. The transmission of interest rate cuts to bank lending and deposit rates is also sluggish in normal times (Hofmann and Mizen, 2004, Craig and Dinger, 2011).

Recent experiences suggest that policy rate cuts below zero generally do transmit to bank lending rates, but sluggishly, and cross-country differences are important. In the Eurozone, the average interest rate on new short-term bank loans has fallen by substantially more than policy and market-based rates since the ECB's move to negative deposit rates in June 2014, with declines in almost all of the member states (ECB, 2016). Interpreting these movements is complicated by the fact that this period also saw the introduction of QE in the Eurozone, which was extended to include bonds rated as low as BBB.

In Denmark and Sweden, bank lending rates have also declined, but more slowly.[19] The sluggishness of transmission to lending rates suggests that banks may be attempting to partly recover costs of the negative interest rate on their deposits at the central bank, and the expensive retail deposit funding, by cross-subsidising these with the lending business. If so, it may be a temporary phenomenon as competition from institutions with different funding characteristics, such as mortgage-backed securitisation pools, compete away the excess spreads. It may also partly reflect that market rates have recently increased in these countries on the back of improving economic prospects.

---

17 There are a few exceptions: FIH bank in Denmark (under resolution) and Alternative Bank in Switzerland have applied moderately negative rates to retail deposits. It seems that Alternative Bank did not lose many customers in the following months.
18 Bank managers express concern that they will lose retail customers if they charge negative interest rates on retail deposits (Cecchetti and Schoenholtz, 2016). Retail customers may suffer from money illusion to a higher degree than institutional or corporate clients, and hence may be less forgiving of a negative interest rate.
19 See Danmarks Nationalbank (2016) and Figure 2.7 in the supporting slides to Sveriges Riksbank (2016).

Switzerland is noteworthy in that bank lending rates for mortgages at longer maturities initially increased when the SNB introduced negative policy rates (Figure 3.7), as the mark-up of mortgage rates over similar-maturity market interest rates widened.[20] Mortgage rates have subsequently dropped, but these drops have largely reflected drops in long-term market rates rather than a drop in the mark-up over these rates. Other Swiss lending and deposit rates have not substantially changed. The sluggish transmission to Swiss bank rates contrasts with the movements in Swiss market rates (Figure 3.6), and the normally positive correlation of policy rates and lending rates. It could be related to the fact that bank funding relies more on deposits in Switzerland than in other countries (Shin, 2016). The cost of not being able to pass on negative rates to deposit rates weighs relatively more on Swiss banks. Another factor may be that banks intermediate mortgages on their own books to a higher degree in Switzerland than in other countries, where market-based funding of mortgages is more common. This may imply a different competitive environment for bank mortgage rates. The transmission of negative interest rates through mortgage rates may be stronger in economies with more market-based mortgage financing, such as Denmark and the United States.

**Figure 3.7** Switzerland: bank interest rates

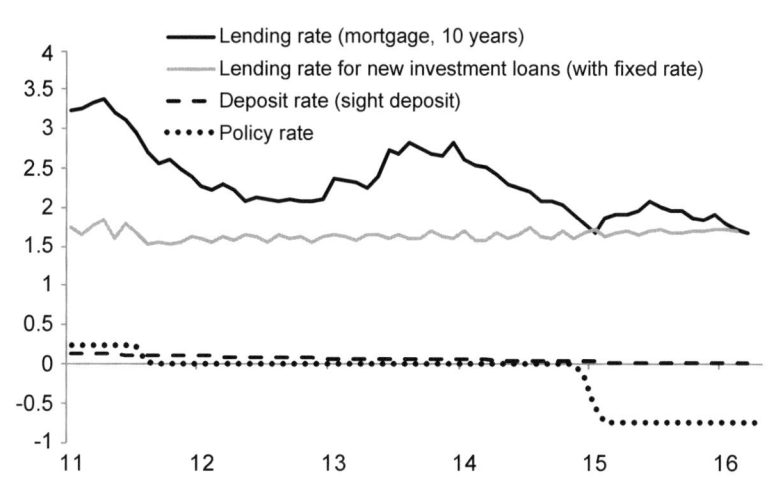

*Sources:* Haver Analytics and SNB.

*Transmission to exchange rates*

The exchange rate transmission channel is particularly relevant for small open economies, where it is typically the most important transmission channel, also in normal times. Exchange rates respond to interest rate differentials between countries. The interest differential is independent of the level of the nominal interest rate, and there is no reason in principle why the exchange rate response to the interest differential should change when the nominal interest rate turns

---

20 Banks usually price mortgages off the interest rate swap curve, which represents the hedged funding cost of a mortgage. The 10-year fixed rate on interest rate swaps largely follow the 10-year Swiss government bond yield, and this has also been the case since the introduction of the negative interest rate.

negative. The scarce evidence suggests that exchange rates have indeed responded to differentials involving negative interest rates in a manner similar to their typical response, and that this channel of transmission is functioning normally with negative rates.

Danmarks Nationalbank's cuts into negative territory did coincide with a fall in the pressure on the krone, as would be expected from a cut in the interest differential. Since the Danish krone is pegged to the euro, this was manifested in a significant reduction in Danmarks Nationalbank's foreign exchange reserves in the months following the imposition of the negative rate (Rohde, 2015).

Most of the announcements of negative interest rates were accompanied by simultaneous announcements of other measures, and the response of the exchange rate to these announcements hence cannot be fully assigned to the negative interest rate. There are two exceptions: the Bank of Japan's surprise announcement of a cut in the marginal deposit rate to −10 basis points in January 2016, and the surprise cut by the Riksbank of a further 15 basis points in February 2016. Both of these announcements were associated with an immediate depreciation of the domestic currency, as market participants reacted as usual to surprise interest rate announcements. The subsequent depreciation of the Swedish krona has been persistent. In the case of Japan, the depreciation was brief. The yen has been on an appreciating trend due to safe haven flows and other factors; a cut of only 10 basis points should not be expected to counter this trend for long (Perli et al., 2016). Moreover, the unexpected cut below zero in Japan proved to be controversial and resulted in market upheaval, which may have increased risk aversion and safe haven pressures, and may have led to market expectations that the Bank of Japan would not cut rates any further. The experience suggests that central bank communication that prepares markets in advance for negative rates may help improve transmission of the measure.

Some central banks have put more emphasis on the exchange rate channel than usual when justifying interest rate cuts into negative territory, and this has led some to conclude that negative interest rates are predominantly a beggar-thy-neighbour policy, perhaps even associated with currency wars. However, interest rate cuts into negative territory work largely in the same way as cuts in positive territory do, and transmit through similar channels. The exchange rate channel is a standard feature of monetary policy transmission, and an important channel for small open economies also in normal times. Monetary policy with negative interest rates is no more a beggar-thy-neighbour policy, and has no more international spillovers, than monetary policy in normal times.

*Do interest rate cuts still transmit to the real economy when rates are negative?*

Recent experience has shown that, even when short-term policy rates are at or close to zero, it is still possible to lower them further, thereby pushing down longer-term rates and real rates and depreciating the exchange rate. Will cuts below zero also be effective in expanding aggregate demand, bringing inflation back in line with objectives and restoring output and employment to potential in a post-financial crisis world? Basic principles point to spending as depending on real rather than nominal interest rates, and there is ample evidence on the impact of real rates. Previous US recessions, for example, have been met with sharp reductions in real policy rates to as low as –4% or –5% (Ball, 2013). These cuts in real rates to levels much lower than at present spurred strong economic recoveries (Romer and Romer, 1994). There is little reason to doubt that reducing

real rates now or in future would have similar effects. Even if the financial sector of an economy is in deleveraging mode following an implosion of financial excesses, sufficient monetary stimulus should work on the margin to stimulate interest sensitive consumption and investment demand. In other words, the IS curve may have shifted down due to negative shocks, deleveraging and higher risk aversion, but it still has a slope. The neutral real interest rate is temporarily reduced, but this means that real interest rate cuts may help counter the effects of these negative shocks on demand. In the last comparable period of financial market disruption and debt overhang in the United States, the mid-1930s monetary expansion was fully effective (Romer, 1992).

Drawing on the model discussed above in Section 2, Box 3.1 presents simulations of how the US economy would have fared had it lowered interest rates below zero in the Great Recession.

The recent cuts below zero were small, and one would not have expected a great boost from such timid policy rate cuts if they had happened in positive territory. The cuts have also been small in comparison to the drops in inflation expectations that they were responding to, and the associated net drops in real rates have therefore tended to be even smaller that the nominal rate cuts.[21] All in all, it would be better to describe the interest rate measures of the past couple of years as having prevented a tightening of monetary conditions and a stronger slowdown, rather than having represented an actual loosening or an active boost to demand.

---

**Box 3.1**   Revisiting the simulations with a negative interest rate

In Section 2, we examined how the Great Recession would have been different if there were no zero bound on interest rates, and compared it to actual experience in which rates stayed non-negative. Here we present simulations that add an intermediate case: the nominal interest rate has a lower bound of –2%. These simulations capture what might have happened if central banks aggressively pushed rates below zero from the start of the recession, but with some limits on how negative policy rates could go (reflecting the alternative of cash).

As we see in Figure 3.8, the fed funds rate would have hit the new lower bound of –2%, but it would have been stuck there for only 10 quarters instead of 28 quarters. The unemployment rate would have been about 0.7 percentage points lower on average starting in 2010, for a cumulative reduction in the unemployment gap of about 4 percentage points. Inflation would have been slightly higher.

---

21  In the Swiss case, for example, the move to negative rates occurred shortly after an appreciation of the exchange rate, which reduced actual and expected inflation substantially in the short to medium term. The decreases in nominal rates and expected inflation had offsetting effects on real rates, leaving these roughly unchanged. With that outcome, and a less competitive exchange rate, one would not expect to see a strengthening of the economy.

**Box 3.1** (contd.)

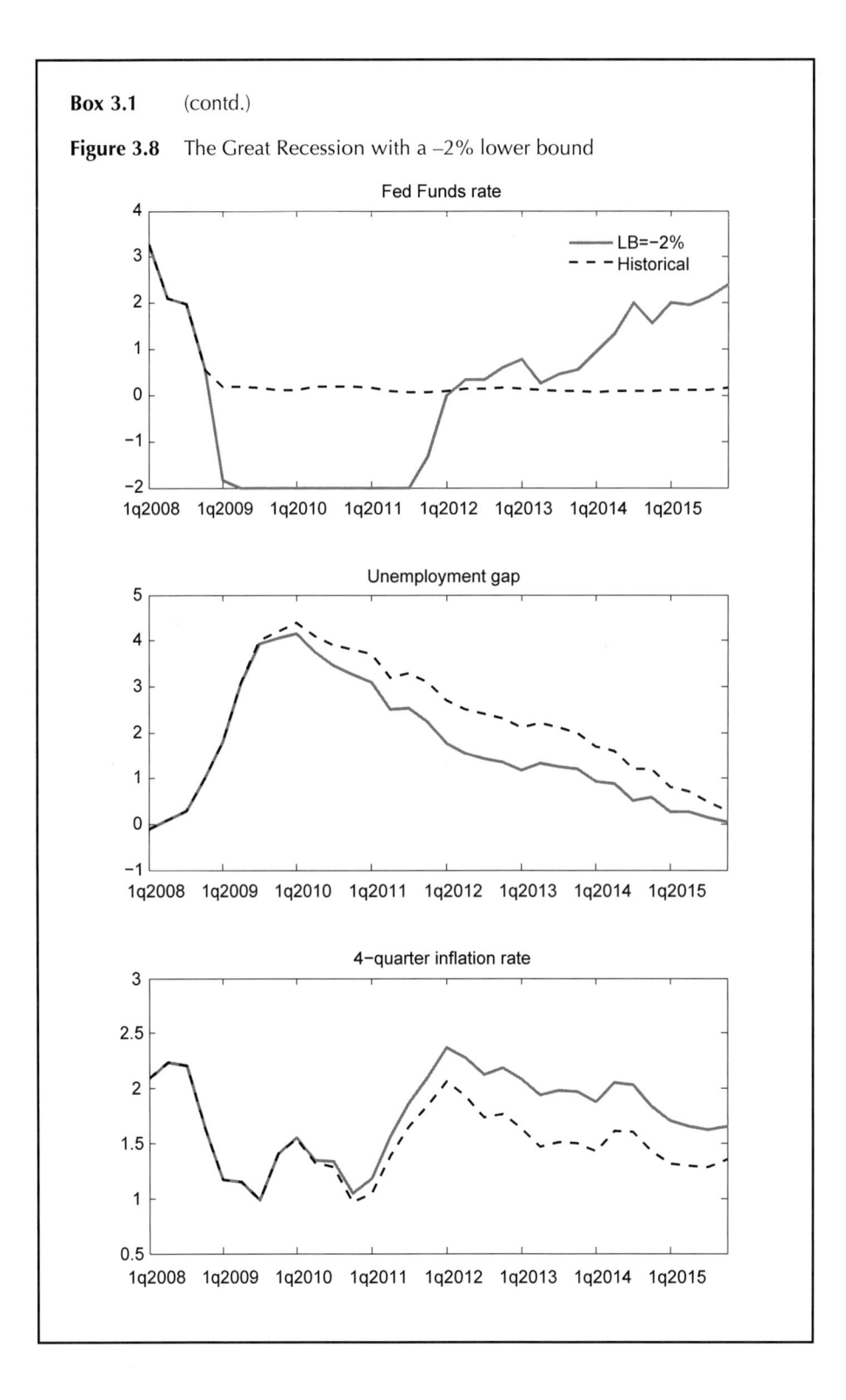

**Figure 3.8** The Great Recession with a −2% lower bound

Could the transmission of real interest rates to economic activity change when nominal rates turn negative? To the extent that households and firms suffer from money illusion, a move to negative rates could be especially powerful in encouraging borrowing. On the other hand, translating the implicit inflation tax on savings into an explicit interest tax might have a negative psychological effect. Moreover, money illusion could exaggerate the pro-saving income effect; indeed, some have argued that income effects could outweigh substitution effects for household savings when nominal rates turn negative. Income effects of interest rate cuts are always present, however, and there is no evidence that they have become stronger with negative interest rates. On balance, there are no strong grounds to predict the net impact of a move into negative nominal interest rates on the interest sensitivity of savings and investment.

A key channel for transmission is growth in bank credit. Figure 3.9 depicts aggregate bank credit growth for Denmark, the Eurozone, Sweden and Switzerland. Keeping in mind the lack of a counterfactual, it shows that credit growth has not responded adversely to negative rates, as would be expected if the interest sensitivity of savings had switched sign. With the exception of Switzerland, where credit growth started moderating already before the introduction of negative interest rates, credit growth has not declined on average during the recent negative interest rate episodes.[22] Although credit growth declined in Denmark during the negative rate period of 2012-13, the experience was similar in the Eurozone, which did not have negative rates at that time. In the Eurozone, moreover, credit growth has picked up since the imposition of negative interest rates.

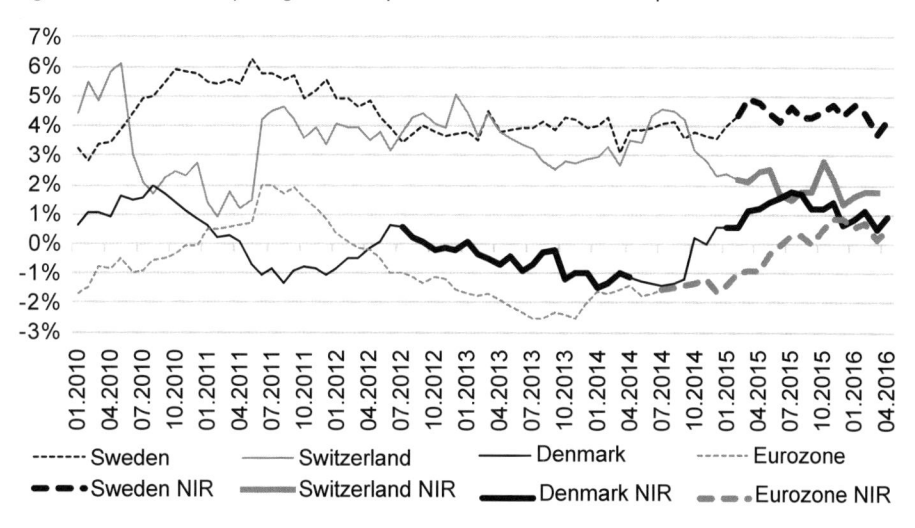

**Figure 3.9**  Year-on-year growth in private domestic credit in percent

*Source:* IMF International Financial Statistics, line 32D (line 22D for Sweden).

---

22  The negative interest rate economies are primarily bank-based economies, and bank credit remains the most relevant credit measure. We could also have looked at net issuance of bonds as an alternative to bank credit. According to data provided by the SNB (online data portal), the net issuance of Swiss franc bonds by Swiss residents significantly increased since interest rates were reduced in the aftermath of the financial crisis, and net issuance has remained at these higher levels in 2015, with no signs that the negative interest rate may be hampering issuance.

Apart from money illusion, the response of bank lending to interest rate cuts could change when interest rates turn negative due to the bank frictions discussed previously. As remarked by Shin (2016), lower bank capital can result in lower bank lending, and if negative interest rates result in reduced bank profitability and retained earnings, this could be relevant. While such concerns cannot be dismissed, they should not be overstated. As discussed in more detail in Section 3.1.4, the medium-term impact on bank profits of a period of negative interest rates is not necessarily negative. Indeed, there has not been much of a reduction in bank profitability so far since the introduction of negative interest rates.

That said, it is too soon to expect comprehensive and conclusive empirical evidence isolating the macroeconomic impact of the negative interest rate policy from the experience of these five central banks.

### 3.1.3 How low can rates go?

How low can policy rates go before banks, firms, and households shift their holdings of liquid assets into cash on a scale that prevents further policy rate transmission?

In considering this question, it is important to distinguish between the transactions demand for liquid assets and the 'store of wealth' demand. For banks, firms and other institutions, physical currency is more costly for transactions than electronic payments.[23] Banks and firms are likely to continue to use electronic money for payments even with deeply negative interest rates. For households, evidence suggests that the sensitivity to transaction costs associated with different means of payments is high.[24] Any large-scale shift to using cash for transactions likely would show up in the retail sector first.

Most banks and firms, and some households, have far more liquid assets than they need for payments purposes. These assets are basically a convenient and safe store of wealth. Any large-scale switch to cash by banks and firms would start with holdings of liquid assets not needed for transactions over the short to medium term. Switching to a large stock of cash incurs set-up costs, ongoing costs of safe storage and, prospectively, a wind-down cost at some future date when it becomes attractive to hold other assets. The decision to make this switch will be influenced by uncertainty about the duration and magnitude of negative interest rates (Dixit, 1989). These considerations likely explain why institutional depositors have continued to hold negative-yielding deposits. The further the move into negative territory and the longer it is expected to last, the more likely depositors are to incur the set-up costs of shifting towards a cash-dominated strategy. It is difficult to determine at what point the shift into cash would get to a sufficiently large scale to hamper monetary policy transmission.

To date, no large-scale shift into cash has occurred. Various estimates of the costs of shifting into cash have been suggested. The ongoing cost of holding cash depends primarily on insurance costs, storage facilities, and security. Figures as high as 35 to 50 basis points have been cited (Burke et al., 2010; Witmer and Yang, 2015), but lower figures have also been mentioned.[25] It is not clear to what extent these estimates fully include the set-up costs involved in building

---

23 Estimates of the inconvenience premium for using cash in retail payments range around 1-2% (Schmeidel et al., 2012; Norges Bank, 2014; Segendorf and Wretman, 2015).
24 Usage of debit cards is quite sensitive to the fee associated with use of that card relative to other cards or cash.
25 Bentow (2015) cites an offer to store cash for 14 basis points in Denmark.

up the capacity to store large amounts of cash. On the other hand, Cecchetti and Schoenholtz (2016) argue that insurance costs of storing cash are likely to increase disproportionately with the amount of cash to store. Another factor discouraging large-scale shifts into cash by financial institutions may be moral suasion by central banks in countries with negative interest rates. We have heard reports of such moral suasion but have found no documentary evidence of its existence or any way to calibrate its potential effect.

**Figure 3.10**  Ratio of the value of the largest denomination of bank notes outstanding to total outstanding bank notes in selected countries, year-end

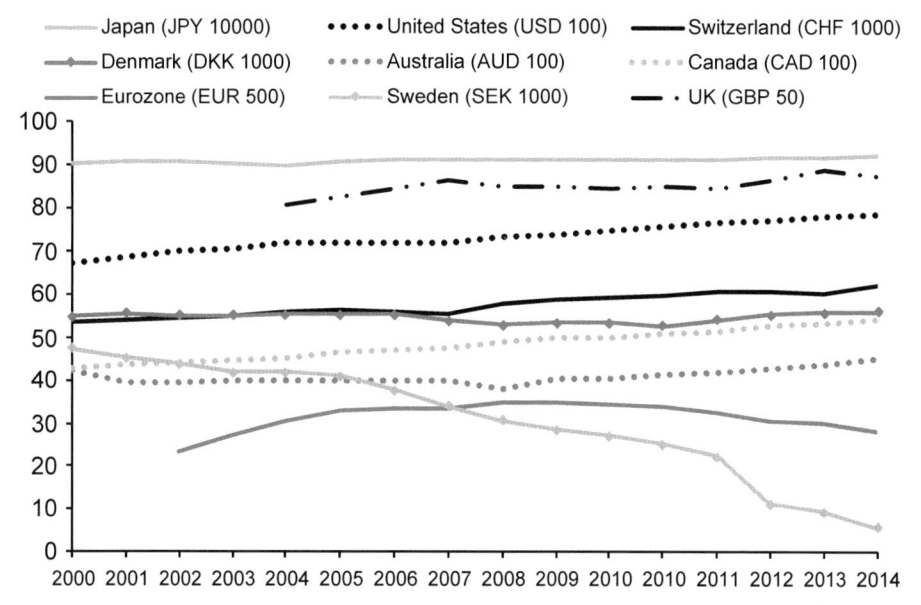

*Note:* The denomination of the largest outstanding banknote is in parenthesis after country labels.
*Sources:* National central banks.

If demand for cash as a store of wealth were to increase, we would expect to see an increase in the relative demand for the largest denomination bank notes. Indeed, ceasing to issue large denomination bank notes is a simple way of increasing the cost of a shift to cash.[26] Figure 3.10 traces the shares of the largest denomination bank note in total bank notes for several countries (including all five negative interest rate countries) since 2000. There has been a small uptick in the share for Denmark since 2012, and Switzerland in 2015, but these are within the normal variation for these countries. In all countries, cash demand has been remarkably stable since the introduction of negative interest rates.[27]

---

26  In most countries, large-denomination banknotes are rarely used for legal payments. Phasing out these banknotes would help in the fights against crime, terrorism and tax evasion (Rogoff, 2014; Sands, 2016; Summers, 2016).
27  We use yearly data here because it allows for the widest cross country sample. Monthly data for the relevant countries reflect the same picture (see, for example, the SNB data portal.

In light of the potentially important fixed cost in setting up cash storage capacity, any large-scale switch to cash likely would respond to both the magnitude of negative interest rates and their expected duration. Market expectations for short-term interest rates in all five countries are negative for the next few years. For example, by early 2016 futures on short-term euro interest rates suggested ECB deposit rates were expected to remain negative until at least the third quarter of 2019. Of the five negative interest countries, Switzerland has the most negative policy rate of –0.75%, and futures on three-month Swiss franc Libor rates have suggested that rates were expected to remain as low for at least three more years. As an illustrative example, suppose the variable cost of storing cash is 0.35% per year. Over the coming three years, the accumulated variable cost of holding cash would amount to 1.05%. Meanwhile, the approximate cumulated nominal interest penalty of a three-month interbank deposit implied by futures rates is a total of 2.25%. The accumulated variable benefit to shifting from holding funds in money markets to holding cash would hence be 1.20% over three years. Since we still do not see a shift into cash, this may imply that the fixed cost of a move into cash is higher than this number in Switzerland. It may in fact be significantly higher. Futures on Swiss franc Libor rates do not increase over the three-year horizon for which we have data, suggesting that they may be expected to remain negative for even longer. It could, on the other hand, also suggest that the variable cost of storing cash is much higher in Switzerland than estimates suggested by the literature.

If a more deeply negative interest rate could push economies out of the lower bound faster than currently expected, it is possible that it might not lead to greater cumulative interest rate penalties, and thus might not raise the probability of a large-scale switch to cash. For example, a rate of –0.75% for three years would imply largely the same cumulated interest penalty as a rate of –2.25% for one year with a zero interest rate for the following two years. The deeper the rate cut, the shorter the likely duration of the recession. Accordingly, the current level of negative interest rates need not represent the lower bound as defined by a large-scale shift into cash.

If a large increase in the demand for cash becomes increasingly likely at a time where a tightening through an interest rate rise would be premature and costly, a central bank might impose higher fees for supplying cash. In order to prevent large-scale cash hoarding, the fees would need to be proportional to the amount withdrawn. Banks would pass these fees on to their customers. The economic disruption would be minimal, as households and firms would be able to use their accounts for electronic payments without any fee or restriction (beyond the negative interest rate). However, such fees likely would be highly unpopular and could expose the central bank to severe political pressure.[28]

Perhaps the strongest de facto impediment to cutting rates further into negative territory is the lack of public acceptance and understanding of such measures. Partly due to pervasive money illusion, negative interest rates seem counterintuitive to the general public and are perceived in many countries as an unfair tax on savings. Taking measures to allow negative retail deposit rates could sharply increase public animosity. A lack of acceptance and understanding of a monetary policy measure can negatively affect confidence in the central

---

[28] Kimball (2016) proposes alternatives to simple fees on cash, and Danthine (2016) proposes a scheme that prevents banks from passing on negative interest rates to depositors while the central bank can move wholesale and market rates increasingly negative.

bank's ability to pursue its mandate, and might adversely affect transmission to demand. This constitutes an important communication challenge for central banks as they try to explain why the tool is needed, how it works, and how negative nominal rates will affect real life-time saving and real incomes of regular citizens, once growth and inflation developments are taken into account. The experience with negative interest rates so far suggests that it may be a good idea to communicate preemptively on these issues, before introducing negative rates. There is no reason to suppose that a surprise announcement of negative interest rates would have greater effects than an expected introduction of negative interest rates. The success and effectiveness of a policy involving negative interest rates is likely to be enhanced if financial markets have been prepared for it.

### 3.1.4 Adverse effects on financial markets and institutions

Financial stability and other policy considerations could also limit the extent to which nominal interest rates can be lowered. While one should not be complacent about these, our review of the nature of the main financial stability concerns highlights the extent to which they should be seen as reflecting transitional issues that can be addressed to allow financial markets to function well with negative rates. They should not constrain monetary policy, but they do highlight the importance of measures to ensure that markets and financial institutions remain resilient in the face of persistently low interest rates.

In the current low interest rate environment, long-term asset managers such as pension and insurance funds often struggle to find assets with the necessary returns to allow them to meet the nominal returns guaranteed on liabilities. Low interest rates could induce some asset managers to take on excessive risk (search for yield) and ultimately result in socially damaging failures of some such institutions. Many firms are taking account of this situation by moving toward business models that are more resilient to protracted deviations in interest rates from their long-term average or expected levels. Pension funds have been shifting toward defined contributions solutions, and unit-linked insurance is increasingly gaining ground (cf. Bank for International Settlements, 2016). Such changes are unlikely to be fast enough to protect the sector fully from the pressures resulting from current low interest rates.

Note, however, that this problem is due to the secular downward trend in real interest rates, and not to accommodating monetary policy or negative nominal interest rates *per se*. Raising nominal interest rates in order to counteract this problem would also raise real interest rates, damaging growth and delaying the prospects for a return to sustainably higher real interest rates.

Banks' net interest margins have narrowed as interest rates have declined since the Global Crisis. The decline in net interest margins is partly driven by the secular downward trend in neutral real interest rates, and not simply by monetary policy or negative interest rates. However, negative nominal interest rates may add to the squeeze of net interest margins, to the extent that they are not transmitted to deposit rates.

Narrowing interest margins do represent a negative for bank profitability, but it can be offset by an expansion of lending volumes as economic activity recovers. Furthermore, the sources of profit in bank business models extend beyond the interest margin. Empirically, narrowing interest margins have not so far been associated with reduced overall bank profitability (Claessens et al., 2016). The

experience in negative interest rate countries to date is that banks have offset the narrowing of margins with higher lending volumes, higher fees and charges, lower loan-loss provisioning, higher capital gains, and lower non-deposit funding costs. In 2015, banks in negative interest rate countries invariably had high profitability, despite nominal interest rates at their lowest levels ever (Danmarks Nationalbank, 2015b; Coeuré, 2016a; Sveriges Riksbank, 2016; UBS, 2016).[29]

If a short spell of negative interest rates were to boost the economy and speed the return to positive interest rates, this should ultimately boost bank profitability. If monetary policy cannot be made sufficiently accommodating to achieve a speedy return because of the lower bound on interest rates, however, the effect of protractedly low interest rates on banks margins could eventually start weighing on overall bank profitability.[30] This would be the result of insufficient stimulus, or a lack of other policies to achieve a sustainable increase in potential growth, however. It would not be advisable to bring nominal interest rates back to positive territory in order to achieve higher bank profitability in the absence of a return to growth, as this would further dampen growth prospects and hence bank profitability. Rather, this scenario again underlines the need for more stimulus – alternative monetary tools, or fiscal and structural policies – to boost growth faster.

Of course, negative interest rates affect banks' profitability differently depending on their business models. Banks that rely more on retail deposits for their funding, and derive the main part of their income from margin business, may see a more adverse effect from negative rates. One way of limiting the direct impact of negative rates on banks' earnings is to apply the negative rates only to the marginal tier of banks' deposits at the central bank. This approach has been adopted in Denmark, Switzerland and Japan,[31] where a large part of central bank reserves are exempted from the negative interest rate, and in some cases receive a positive interest rate.[32] Such exemption systems can be challenged as an unfair subsidy to banks, and they are very hard to design in a way that does not discriminate some bank business models over others, but they should not reduce the incentive for banks to transmit the negative interest rate to bank deposits and loans.

An often-voiced concern about adverse effects of negative rates derives from the commitment of money market mutual funds (MMMFs) not to 'break the buck' (McAndrews, 2015), making them subject to a run when returns threaten to be negative. These concerns are met by new regulatory initiatives requiring that most MMMFs move to a floating net asset value regime, both in the US and

---

29  See also Coeuré (2016b). Even in Germany, often cited as an economy whose banking system has much to lose from negative interest rates, the projected impact of a protracted period of negative interest rates on bank profits and bank capital is modest (IMF, 2016).

30  In general, accommodative monetary policy has been linked to a reduction in bank profitability (Borio et al., 2015a). This effect is not specific to negative interest rates, but rather reflects subdued interest rate expectations as well as a low term premium.

31  The Bank of Japan has refined this approach by creating a three-tier system of interest on reserves, as opposed to a two-tier system in Denmark and Switzerland. The first lump-sum tranche of Japanese banks' reserves receives a positive interest rate, while the middle tranche has zero interest. Only the upper tranche is subject to a negative interest rate. It is the rate on this upper tranche that binds on the margin for banks, and this rate that hence transmits to the markets. The Bank of Japan can use the positive-interest tranche to channel back to the banks – in a lump-sum fashion – a transfer that offsets most of the effect of the negative rate on average bank profitability.

32  Banks do not benefit from shifting their assets into cash as long as banks' cash holdings are deducted from the part of deposits that are exempt from the negative rate, as is the case in Switzerland and Japan.

in Europe.[33] The initial experience with negative interest rates in Europe is that MMMFs are coping well with negative short-term yields, and have been able to shift to negative yields without disruptions or redemptions (ECB, 2015).

Some legal and software modifications have been needed to ensure that financial firms, including financial market trading platforms and other infrastructures, can cope with negative interest rates (Fischer, 2016). It is desirable that the necessary adjustments (for example, in tax laws) be put in place ahead of time. But in practice the necessary fixes have been accomplished in the relevant countries without insurmountable difficulty.[34]

More generally, given the possibility that neutral real interest rates will stay low or move even lower in the future (Bean et al., 2015), the business models of all financial institutions need to be refined to make them more resilient to variable or low interest rates.

In short, the recent experience has tended to dispel many of the practical and policy concerns that existed around the move to negative monetary policy interest rates. Of course, there is a limit to how low rates can go and for how long. That limit has not yet been reached. The lower the rate, the faster the economic recovery, and the shorter the time needed for keeping interest rates low or negative. Central banks can push rates negative to some extent without triggering a sharp shift into cash. Nevertheless, such policies bring central banks into uncharted territory and they need to watch for signs that such a shift is imminent. Pushing rates beyond the point that induces a large-scale switch to cash would be counterproductive and would force central banks to move into reverse.

## 3.2 Quantitative easing

Quantitative easing (QE) consists of large-scale purchases of existing assets or extensions of new credit by the central bank. The most common form of QE is purchases of long-term government, or government-guaranteed, bonds. We focus most of our analysis on this type of QE. However, central banks also have purchased private bonds, equities, and real estate investment trusts. In addition, central banks have conducted low-cost or subsidised lending programmes targeted at boosting credit creation. The channels by which these programmes affect the economy differ to some extent, but they all share the features of (1) expanding the central bank's balance sheet, and (2) reducing funding costs and increasing credit availability to some sectors of the economy.

---

33  For US regulatory initiatives, see Securities and Exchange Commission (2014). The rule on floating net asset value is to be implemented by October 2016. New US regulation also gives MMMFs the possibility to apply fees and gates to redemptions in times of liquidity stress, which should further increase their ability to manage high redemptions without such events spilling over into systemic events. For EU regulatory initiatives, see the article in the *Financial Times*, "EU money funds spring regulatory leak", 28 June 2015.
34  For example, when interest rates on floating rate mortgage loans and the related bonds turned negative in Denmark, the practical problems were handled expeditiously, using a mechanism that writes-down outstanding values at redemption, instead of reversing coupon payment flows (see https://www.evm.dk/english/news/2015/15-05-06-negative-mortgage-rates).

Central banks pay for QE by issuing highly liquid liabilities.[35] Through the interest rate it pays on these liabilities, the central bank effectively sets the economy-wide level of the short-term risk-free interest rate.[36] For analytical clarity (and consistent with recent practice), in our discussion of the effectiveness of QE, the central bank is assumed to hold its short-term policy rate fixed when conducting QE. QE in conjunction with a change in the short-term rate can be analysed as a combination of pure QE and conventional monetary policy.

### 3.2.1 Recent use and effectiveness of quantitative easing

As policy rates became constrained by the lower bound in the wake of the Global Crisis, the Federal Reserve, the Bank of England, the ECB, the Bank of Japan, and Sweden's Riksbank undertook large-scale purchases of long-term bonds.[37] The Bank of Japan also purchased small amounts of equity and real estate. The Bank of England, the Bank of Japan, and the ECB also set up programmes of lending on concessional terms to boost bank credit. Gagnon and Hinterschweiger (2013) describe the timing and nature of these programs (as of December 2012) in more detail.

The empirical literature assessing the effectiveness of QE programmes is remarkably consistent in pointing to a successful transmission of such programmes to nominal long-term yields and asset prices. QE has worked to lower real interest rates through a reduction in nominal yields and term spreads. This reduction in real rates is likely to have provided substantial stimulus to the real economy (see also Box 3.2).

The fact that QE to a large extent works through a reduction in term premiums suggests that it could have an effect on bank profitability connected to maturity transformation (Borio et al., 2015a), which could hamper transmission if bank lending is adversely affected. But in the two large countries with the longest recent experience of QE, there is not much sign of lower bank profitability resulting from QE. In the United States, bank profitability has been strong since 2011, with return on assets of 1%, close to its historical average since 1984.[38] In the United Kingdom, while bank profits are down noticeably, declining net interest margins are only a small factor; more important seem to be regulatory changes that reduce bank trading and risk taking behaviour (Bank of England, 2015).

---

35  In principle, central banks could issue long-term liabilities. In practice, central banks rarely do so. Issuing long-term liabilities would reduce the effect of QE on the term premium of interest rates.
36  In regimes in which interest is not paid on central bank liabilities and short-term interest rates are guided by the scarcity of these liabilities, a significant expansion of central bank assets quickly eliminates the scarcity value of central bank liabilities and pushes market interest rates close to zero.
37  The Bank of Japan also conducted large bond purchases in 2001-05, but this earlier QE programme was limited to short-term government bonds and had relatively minor effects.
38  Data are from the FRED database of the Federal Reserve Bank of St. Louis.

**Box 3.2** Simulation of the effect of US quantitative easing in the Great Recession

Here we present further simulations of our simple model (introduced above in Section 2) to show how the Great Recession might have developed in the United States if the Fed had not conducted QE. The dashed lines in Figure 3.11 display historical data; the solid line displays our simulation of no QE. We implement the simulation by adding a long-term interest rate to the model (details are in the appendix.) The long-term interest rate responds by one-quarter of any movement in the short-term interest rate plus an exogenous term premium. Based on the work of Engen et al. (2015), we assume that QE reduced the term premium by 50 basis points in 2009 and 2010, with the effect growing in steps to a 125 basis point reduction in 2013-15.

Under both simulations, the fed funds rate is stuck at the zero lower bound from 2009Q1 onward. The long-term rate with no QE gradually rises relative to its historical value. The unemployment gap comes down much more slowly than in the historical data, so that unemployment is about 1.5 percentage points higher than its historical level in late 2015. (This is a bit larger than the results of Engen et al., who find that QE reduced the unemployment rate just over 1 percentage point as of 2015Q1.) Core inflation is also further below target in the simulation with no QE.

Although we do not show results in these plots, the model implies that a larger magnitude of QE, and hence a lower term premium, would have pushed unemployment down faster and kept inflation higher than the historical outcome.

**Figure 3.11** Great Recession with and without quantitative easing

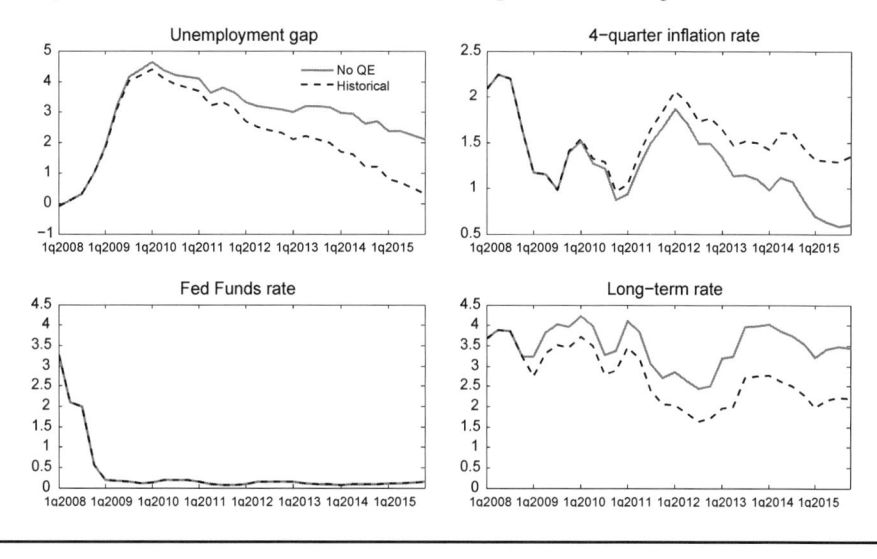

## 34  What Else Can Central Banks Do?

**Table 3.1**  Estimated effects of quantitative easing on 10-year bond yields

| Study | Sample | Method | Yield reduction (basis points) |
|---|---|---|---|
| **United States** | | | |
| Greenwood and Vayanos (2008)[a] | 1952-2005 | Time series | 82 |
| Gagnon, Raskin, Remache & Sack (2011) | 2008-09 | Event study | 78 |
|  | 1985-2007 | Time series TP only | 44 |
| Krishnamurthy & Vissing-Jorgensen (2011) | 2008-09 | Event study | 91 |
|  | 2010-11 | Event study | 47 |
| Hamilton & Wu (2012) | 1990-2007 | Affine model | 47 |
| Swanson (2011) | 1961 | Event study | 88 |
| D'Amico & King (2013) | 2009-10 | Micro event study | 240 |
| D'Amico, English, Lopez-Salido & Nelson (2012) | 2002-08 | Weekly time series | 165 |
| Li & Wei (2012) | 1994-2007 | Affine model of TP | 57 |
| Rosa (2012) | 2008-10 | Event study | 42 |
| Neely (2012) | 2008-09 | Event study | 84 |
| Bauer & Neely (2012) | 2008-09 | Event study | 80 |
| Bauer & Rudebusch (2011)[b] | 2008-09 | Event study TP only | 44 |
| Christensen & Rudebusch (2012)[b] | 2008-09 | Event study TP only | 26 |
| Chadha, Turner & Zampolli (2013) | 1990-2008 | Time series TP only | 56 |
| Swanson (2015)[b] | 2009-15 | Yield curve TP only | 40 |
| Christensen & Rudebusch (201d)[b] | 2008-09 | Event study TP only | 15 |
| **United Kingdom** | | | |
| Joyce, Lasaosa, Stevens & Tong (2011) | 2009 | Event study | 78 |
|  | 1991-2007 | Time series | 51 |
| Christensen & Rudebusch (2012)[b] | 2009-11 | Event study TP only | 34 |
| Churm, Joyce, Kapetanios & Theodoris (2015 | 2011-12 | Intl. comparison | 42 |
| **Japan** | | | |
| Fukunaga, Kato & Koeda (2015) | 1992-2014 | Time series TP only | 24 |
|  | 2013-14 | Event study | 17 |
| **Eurozone** | | | |
| Middeldorp (2015)[c] | 2013-15 | Event study | 45-132 |
| Altavilla, Carboni & Motto (2015)[d] | 2014-15 | Event study | 44 |
| Middeldorp & Wood (2016)[c] | 2015 | Event study | 41-104 |
| **Sweden** | | | |
| De Rezende, Kjellberg & tysklind (2015) | 2015 | Event study | 68 |

*Note:* a. Greenwood & Vayanos scaled the effect relative to the size of the Treasury market. The estimate here is based on the ratio of Treasury debt to GDP in 2015. b These studies further differentiate between signaling effects and portfolio effects. The reported estimate is for the portfolio effect only. c. The smaller estimate is for German bonds and the larger one is for Italian bonds. d. The estimate is for an average of Eurozone bonds.

Purchases normalised to 10% of GDP. There are 100 basis points in 1 percentage point. Most studies present a range of estimates. This table displays the study's preferred estimate if one exists; if not, it presents the midpoint of the range. For event studies, we normalise by purchases of all long-term bonds, not only government bonds. Some of the non-event studies include non-government bond purchases and others do not. "TP only" denotes studies that attempt to estimate the term premium component of movements in bond yields. For event studies, the normalisation is based on GDP in the final year of the event.

*Source:* Gagnon (2016)

*Quantitative easing in bonds*

Many studies find significant effects of QE bond purchases on bond yields (e.g. Williams, 2014; Gagnon, 2016). Table 3.1, taken from Gagnon (2016), displays estimates of the effect of a purchase of long-term bonds equivalent to 10% of GDP on a country's 10-year government bond yield. The median estimate is around 50 basis points. We are not aware of any study that suggests that QE does not affect bond yields. A few studies argue that the effects are transitory, but most find persistent effects. Many studies also find that QE reduces yields on bonds that are not being purchased, such as corporate bonds, and that QE raises equity prices, depreciates the exchange rate, and reduces yields on foreign bonds (Neely, 2012; Rogers et al., 2014).

QE lowers bond yields through three main channels: (1) central bank purchases help to calm markets during a crisis, both by demonstrating that the authorities are determined to help and by providing a credible buyer of last resort; (2) purchases may be viewed as enhancing the credibility of central bank guidance that future policy rates are likely to remain low for a long time (also known as the signalling channel); and (3) purchases reduce the amount of assets with term risk – and in some cases, credit or liquidity risk – that private investors must hold, thereby raising their prices (also known as the portfolio channel).[39]

Some observers have conjectured that QE works only during a panic or that there is a decreasing marginal effect of QE (Summers, 2015). Such views can best be interpreted in terms of the three channels of QE effects. The market-calming channel works only during times of financial stress. The signalling and portfolio channels operate across a wider range of circumstances. However, there are limits to the signalling channel because central banks cannot credibly commit to keeping the policy rate at its lower bound indefinitely; two or three years may be the maximum any central bank can credibly commit to a fixed low policy rate. On the other hand, there is no reason to expect either increasing or decreasing marginal impacts of the portfolio channel.[40]

Bond yields are presumably also subject to a lower bound when they fall sufficiently below zero. Bond holders have the same option as holders of deposits or money market instruments to switch into cash, which provides a fixed long-term yield of zero (and the chance of a capital gain likely diminishes as yields go lower). Longer-term bond yields have turned negative in Switzerland and Japan. As with short-term interest rates, we have yet to test the limits of negative rates on long-term bonds.

Staff at the Fed estimate that actual and expected QE purchases in the United States as of late 2013 reduced the yield on the 10-year Treasury note about 125 basis points (Engen et al., 2015). In order to reduce the 10-year Treasury yield by 125 basis points, the Fed typically would have to lower the federal funds rate by 500 basis points (Chung et al., 2011). However, the macroeconomic effects of a reduction in the long-term yield caused by QE (with a fixed short-term rate) are roughly half as large as the macro effects of the same reduction in the long-term

---

[39] Other channels have been proposed (Krishnamurthy and Vissing-Jorgensen, 2011; Christensen and Krogstrup 2016). We consider these as included in the three broader channels mentioned here.

[40] An increasing marginal effect would arise if the last remaining holders of assets being purchased have highly inelastic demands for these assets and thus require extremely high prices to be induced to sell them. On the other hand, a decreasing marginal effect would arise if central banks attempt to push risk premiums below zero. Note that term premiums are not the same as risk premiums and may go below zero to the extent that certain classes of investors (such as life insurance companies and pension funds) have a strong demand for assets with fixed long-term payoffs.

yield brought about by lowering the short-term policy rate (Kiley, 2014; Chen et al., 2012). Reductions in the short-term rate have a stimulative effect above and beyond their effects on the long-term rate because many loans are indexed to the short-term rate. Accordingly, a 125 basis point decline in the 10-year Treasury yield caused by QE at the zero lower bound has an effect comparable to a 250 basis point decline in the short-term interest rate in normal times.

One study describes the macroeconomic effects of QE using the concept of a 'shadow' short-term rate based on the entire term structure of interest rates and its historical influence on macroeconomic variables.[41] The shadow rate is constructed to be close to the short-term rate in normal times, but can go below zero when the short-term interest rate is stuck at zero. When QE reduces longer-term interest rates, the shadow rate declines, reflecting both the portfolio and signalling channels of QE. Estimates show a shadow short-term interest rate in the United States of around –200 basis points in late 2013, falling to –300 basis points in mid-2014, and returning to around –200 basis points in early 2015 (Wu and Xia, 2014).[42]

Churm et al. (2015) find that the portfolio effects of QE bond purchases in the United Kingdom are equivalent to a cut in the policy rate of around 150 to 300 basis points.

Reviewing the change in financial market conditions as the ECB ramped up its asset purchasing programme, Draghi (2015) noted that between early June 2014 and March 2015 (when the large expansion of the programme and its extension to government securities took effect), the GDP-weighted average of Eurozone 10-year government bond yields fell by around 150 basis points (while the policy interest rate fell by only 20 basis points) "as markets began to price in [the ECB's] likely response to a prolonged period of too-low inflation". Spillover effects were also evident: yields of bank bonds fell, on average, by 75 basis points and investment-grade bonds issued by other firms fell by about 100 basis points over the same period. Indeed, between June 2014 and November 2015, "composite lending rates for non-financial companies have declined by more than 70 basis points for the euro area as a whole, and by between 110 and 120 basis points in stressed economies in the euro area periphery". The ECB estimates that a 100 basis point reduction in its policy rate at the start of that period would have been needed to accomplish this degree of financial market easing.[43]

We are not aware of any published analysis of the macroeconomic effects of the Bank of Japan's QE programme since 2013. However, core inflation rose nearly 2 percentage points between early 2013 and late 2015 (see Box 3.3.) Given the weak global economy and the large Japanese consumption tax increase in 2014, we see no plausible explanation for the increase in core inflation besides QE and the Bank of Japan's promise to raise inflation permanently to 2%.

---

41  Other studies of so-called shadow rates focus on financial asset prices without reference to macroeconomic effects.
42  Updated data are available at https://www.frbatlanta.org/cqer/research/shadow_rate.aspx.
43  See Darracq-Paries and de Santis (2013) and Carpenter et al. (2013) for estimates of the effects of earlier non-standard monetary policy measures of the ECB.

*Quantitative easing through targeted lending*

Targeted lending operates through different channels than asset purchases, and it may be a more appropriate form of QE for economies that are heavily reliant on bank financing. Most programmes lend to banks at concessional rates and medium terms based on performance criteria for the amount or types of new bank lending. The Fed's programme lent to special purpose vehicles that packaged auto, credit card and student loans, but it did not provide a concessional rate and the programme was ended in 2010.

The Bank of England's Funding for Lending Scheme subsidises loans up to 150 basis points based on net new lending criteria; the marginal subsidy for some additional lending has been higher because of the way the incentive is structured. Spreads on loans to final customers under the programme appear to have declined by about 100 basis points. The Bank of England estimates that the macroeconomic effect of the programme may be equivalent to a cut in the policy rate of 75 to 150 basis points (Bank of England 2014b, p. 14).

The ECB provided long-term (three-year) funding to banks at the normal policy rate starting in late 2011. Recently it announced a new programme of loans at concessional rates and four-year maturities based on targets for net new bank lending. Rates in the new programme may be as low as the ECB deposit rate of –0.4%, which is well below the marginal cost of term funds for many Eurozone banks.

Since 2013, the Bank of Japan has been gradually expanding a programme of lending on concessional terms for banks that meet criteria for new lending, with an emphasis on objectives such as promoting human and physical capital and rebuilding in disaster areas.

An alternative approach is to encourage the securitisation of loans to free up bank balance sheets for new lending. The ECB purchases a modest amount of such loan packages in the form of covered bonds. The Fed's purchases of mortgage backed securities (MBS) also have this property, but they were guaranteed by federal agencies.

*Quantitative easing in equities and real estate*

Japan has included equity and real estate in its QE programme. No published study has sought to estimate the marginal effect of these elements of QE in Japan, but there is evidence to support a significant positive effect of QE equity purchases on equity prices, and thus on overall spending. In principle, one would expect that printing money to buy risky assets would have a greater macroeconomic effect than printing money to buy comparatively safe government bonds.[44]

The first body of evidence concerns studies of the effect of composition changes in equity price indexes. Equity mutual funds that track a specific equity index must sell shares that are deleted from the index and buy shares that are added to the index. Because these index changes carry no information about the performance of the underlying stocks, they can be considered exogenous shifts in supply as far as other investors are concerned. The associated change in stock price reveals the elasticity of demand of the non-indexed-fund share of the

---

[44] Indeed, some have argued that an important aspect of the Great Recession was a shift in demand toward safer assets. For this reason, central banks should focus QE programmes on reducing risk held by the private sector and not on buying government bonds (Krishnamurthy and Vissing-Jorgensen, 2011; Caballero and Farhi, 2016; Ubide, 2016).

market. For the S&P 500 index, Shleifer (1986) and Petajisto (2009) find average price elasticities of demand close to one. In other words, a reduction of the supply of a stock equal to 1% of its market capitalisation raises its price by 1%.[45]

The second piece of evidence concerns the large purchase of equities by the Hong Kong Monetary Authority (HKMA) during the Asian Financial Crisis. Goodhart and Lu (2003) show that the Hang Seng Index rose 18% over a period of two weeks in which the HKMA bought 7% of its market capitalisation. They also present statistical analysis suggesting that equity prices might otherwise have declined, so that the net effect may have been even greater than the 18% increase. On the other hand, it is possible that the price elasticity of demand was elevated during this period of unusual financial stress, which is widely believed to have included an attack on the Hong Kong stock market by international hedge funds.

An important difference between the studies of equity price index rebalancing and the Hong Kong intervention is that the former episodes did not involve any macroeconomic stimulus, whereas the latter probably was viewed as boosting overall prospects for economic growth in Hong Kong. By its nature, a QE programme of buying equities would be aimed at boosting spending and growth, and thus could have a large reinforcing macroeconomic effect on the level of equity prices. Consequently, it seems likely that a large-scale QE programme of equity purchases, say 10 or 20% of market capitalisation, would raise overall equity prices considerably more than 10 or 20%.

Just as QE purchases of bonds are found to raise equity prices and depreciate exchange rates, QE purchases of equity may be expected to lower bond yields and depreciate exchange rates, though such effects have not yet been studied.

Assuming that QE purchases can raise equity prices, they should stimulate economic activity. In the Fed's FRB/US model of the US economy, both household consumption and business investment respond positively to equity prices, with consumption rising by three cents for each dollar increase in equity wealth. In FRB/US, a 5% sustained increase in the value of the stock market raises GDP by about 0.3 percentage points after a few years. It is possible that this result understates the effect of stock market wealth. Recent research finds a consumption effect of stock market wealth that is twice as large as that in the FRB/US model (Carroll et al., 2011).

### 3.2.2 Scope for additional quantitative easing

There is considerable scope in all advanced countries for additional QE.

*Bonds and loans*

Table 3.2 shows that central banks in the major advanced economies, with the exception of Switzerland, have plenty of scope to purchase additional domestic bonds. (Essentially all of the Swiss central bank's assets, and most of the Korean central bank's assets, are in foreign securities.)

---

[45] Based on a uniquely large rebalancing of the Nikkei 225 index in 2000, Greenwood (2005) finds initial price elasticities much higher than one, but he also finds substantial reversion of prices in subsequent weeks. Uncertainty concerning the underlying causes for subsequent price movements and differences in behaviour of stocks that were added, deleted or down-weighted make it difficult to summarise Greenwood's results in a single, long-run elasticity estimate.

**Table 3.2** Scope for quantitative easing in major advanced economies (2015Q4, percent of GDP)

| | Central bank assets | Total securities | Domestic bonds and international bonds in local currency | | | Stock market |
|---|---|---|---|---|---|---|
| | | | Financial corporations | Non-financial corporations | Government | |
| Australia | 9 | 202 | 58 | 3 | 44 | 97 |
| Canada | 5 | 200 | 22 | 14 | 61 | 103 |
| Eurozone | 26 | 182 | 47 | 9 | 74 | 53 |
| Japan | 77 | 382 | 51 | 13 | 202 | 115 |
| Korea | 30 | 194 | 32 | 36 | 36 | 90 |
| Sweden | 16 | 341 | 54 | 2 | 27 | 257 |
| Switzerland | 98 | 261 | 15 | 3 | 14 | 229 |
| United Kingdom | 22 | 275 | 36 | 11 | 92 | 136 |
| United States | 25 | 300 | 81 | 30 | 90 | 99 |

*Notes:* Stock market capitalisation includes companies listed on national exchanges that may be headquartered in other countries. Australian stock data refer to Australian companies only. Swedish stock data include companies listed on other Nordic and Baltic exchanges. Corporate debt includes government-guaranteed debt, e.g. agency debt and agency MBS in the United States.

*Sources:* Bank for International Settlements, Haver Analytics, IMF and national central banks.

At times, central banks have set themselves limits on the share of any individual security they are willing to hold. For example, the ECB limits its purchases of government bonds to 33% of any issue. But it is not clear how important such limits are or at what level they should be set.[46] Indeed, on 21 April 2016, the ECB announced that it would begin buying as much as 70% of the debt issued by individual non-financial corporations.

Concerns also have been expressed about the rate of purchases. During much of 2009, the Fed was purchasing more than 90% of all newly created MBS in the United States. This massive market presence may have temporarily disrupted the business model of some financial firms, but the market returned to normal functioning immediately at the end of the QE programme with no apparent lasting damage.

In addition to purchases of existing bonds, central banks could expand loans to banks on concessional terms or expand purchases of loans from banks and other financial institutions.

46 One concern is that holding enough of an issue to form a blocking minority in a collective action clause under a default might deter other investors from purchasing that security. But the central bank could promise to vote with the majority of the remaining shareholders. ECB concerns may also relate to the Treaty prohibition on monetary financing of EU governments and the possible interpretation of this prohibition as potentially requiring the ECB to block a negotiated restructuring of one or more government bonds.

## 40  What Else Can Central Banks Do?

*Equity*

Equity market capitalisation in the main advanced economies ranges from 53% of GDP in the Eurozone to more than 200% of GDP in Sweden and Switzerland (Table 3.2). Because companies may be listed on multiple markets, these data overstate the market capitalisation of domestic firms, particularly in Sweden, Switzerland and the United Kingdom. In some countries, market capitalisation is dominated by a few companies.

The Bank of Japan is buying a small amount of equity as part of its QE programme, but it is not clear what the marginal effect is given that most of the programme is focused on government bonds.[47] That said, the Japanese equity market soared in anticipation of, and following, the launch of QE in the country in 2013, as can be seen in Figure 3.12. During the period in which the Bank of England and the Fed were the only central banks pursuing QE policies (March 2009 through March 2013), the UK and US equity markets outperformed those of the Eurozone and Japan.

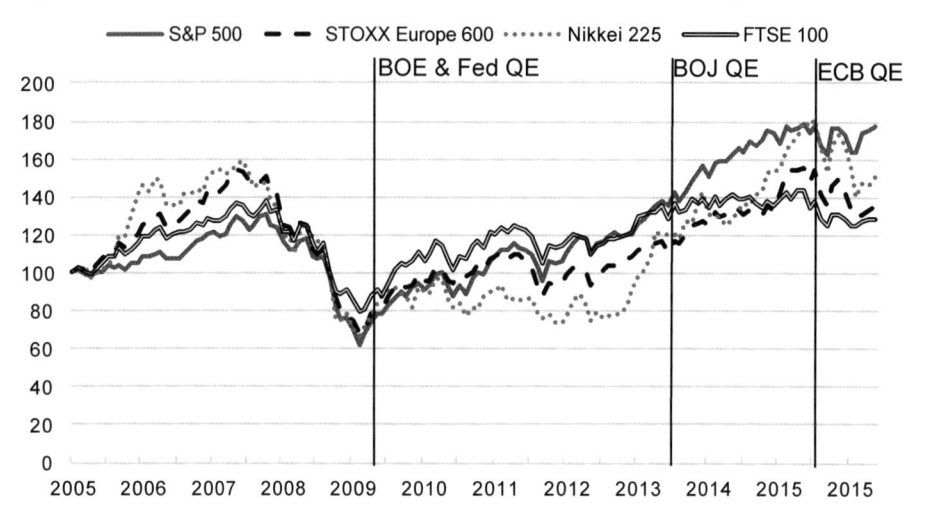

**Figure 3.12** Performance of stock indices, December 2005 to February 2016

The Bank of Japan implements its equity purchases through broad exchange-traded funds (ETFs). Some observers have mistakenly concluded that the current size of ETFs in Japan puts a tight limit on how much the Bank of Japan can buy. In fact, ETF size is endogenous to demand. Purchases of ETF shares cause the ETF management company to purchase more of the underlying equities. The upper size limit of an ETF linked to the Topix index is the market capitalisation of all shares on the Tokyo market.

---

47  Indeed, Japan has a long history of so-called price-keeping operations (PKOs), or equity purchases by the Bank of Japan. A typical motivation for PKOs was to encourage the unwinding of cross-shareholdings among companies or the reduction of bank holdings of equity in periods of low or falling equity prices. Prior to 2013, the Bank of Japan held equity worth 0.4% of GDP (Bank of Japan, 2012). Since 2013, these holdings have increased by 1% of GDP (Bank of Japan, various dates).

*Ordering across assets and exit*

How should a central bank communicate its intention to conduct QE in alternative assets in order to maximise the benefits and minimise market disruption?

The choice of which assets to buy first depends on each country's unique structure and legal framework. As we have seen, QE has started with a focus on long-term bonds, particularly long-term government bonds. In the United States, the Fed is permitted to buy only bonds issued or guaranteed by the federal government, a federal agency, or a foreign government.[48] In countries with a small bond market, on the other hand, it may be best to focus on equities or on subsidised lending.

An alternative approach would be to set the market portfolio as the default QE asset, or even the default central bank asset, at all times. Holding all securities available in proportion to their shares of the overall market would avoid perceptions of unfairness, favouritism or corruption.

There are valid grounds for central banks to retain larger balance sheets than they had before the Great Recession (Gagnon and Sack, 2014). But it is widely agreed that many, if not most, of the QE assets should be allowed to run off eventually. One reason to keep the adjustment gradual is to prevent any disruption of financial markets, particularly in less liquid assets such as the Fed's mortgage-backed securities. Another reason is to establish a precedent that QE purchases are intended to be held for a long time. A QE purchase that is expected to be sold in the near future would have little net effect on financial conditions.

*Managing unintended consequences*

Does central bank ownership of a significant fraction of the economy's productive assets threaten productivity, or have other harmful or beneficial side effects? In an extreme case in which a central bank gained control of more than 50% of corporate bonds and equity, would this be a backdoor nationalisation?

No central bank has come anywhere close to buying a majority of private corporate securities. But even at much lower levels of ownership, a central bank might have effectively a controlling share of many corporations. There are issues concerning voting rights in shares and in bankruptcy courts. One option is to delegate voting to third parties with a clear mandate, or to abstain on such votes and let the other stakeholders decide.[49]

The importance of these concerns rises in proportion with the central bank's ownership share of private assets. A 50% share marks an important threshold of concern. It is unlikely that QE purchases would need to be so high. If additional macroeconomic stimulus were needed when QE assets were already so large, there might be a strong argument for coordinated monetary and fiscal expansion instead of additional purchases of private assets (see Section 3.3 on helicopter money).

---

48 The Fed also may buy US local government bonds with maturities of less than six months. With the approval of the Secretary of the Treasury, the Fed may set up a programme to make secured loans to private corporations that would be similar in effect to buying corporate bonds.

49 Or, if an abstention is counted as a "no", the central bank could vote "yes" if a majority of other shareholders vote "yes". Alternatively, the central bank could vote in a way that it perceives to be in the public's interest or hire professional managers tasked with deciding what is in the public's interest.

Another unintended consequence of QE is its effects on the distribution of wealth. By lowering interest rates (including those on car loans and home mortgages) and increasing total employment, QE undeniably benefits lower-income households, who are more likely to be net borrowers than lenders and are more strongly affected by fluctuations in employment. However, QE does have an important intergenerational effect (Farmer and Zabczyk, 2016). Existing holders of financial assets (mainly older high-income households) enjoy a windfall gain, while savers (mainly younger high-income households) suffer lower expected returns on their saving. However, this intergenerational effect is always present in monetary policy and is not unique to QE.

### 3.2.3 Fiscal implications

Profits have risen strikingly at the Fed and the Bank of Japan since launching QE (Figure 3.13).[50] Economists at the Federal Reserve have shown that the cumulative extra profits the Fed accrued as a result of its QE programmes to date are likely to total around $300 to $400 billion and that the probability the cumulative profits could be negative is essentially zero (Christensen et al., 2015). Indeed, there is only about a 10% chance of having a lower than normal profit in any single year over the life of the programme.

In general, we expect that expanded balance sheets will make central bank profits larger and more variable, reflecting the increase in leverage. Central banks hold assets with greater risk and longer maturities than their liabilities, which have the shortest possible maturities and zero default risk. Thus, expected profits at central banks should normally be positive and increasing in the size of their balance sheets. However, QE may push the term premium on long-term bonds below zero, in which case the marginal expansion of the balance sheet would tend to reduce expected profits.

To the extent that central bank funding costs are more cyclical than the returns on central bank assets, central bank profits are likely to be countercyclical, which provides a natural hedge to the fiscal authority. Countercyclical profits arise because the central bank pushes down the interest rate it pays on its liabilities aggressively in a recession to stimulate spending and other rates of return do not fall as much, in part because private agents become more risk averse in recessions. However, in the four major economies to date, central bank profits (and potential future losses) are small in relation to the swing in fiscal deficits during the Great Recession.

**Table 3.3** Volatility of US financial asset returns, 2000-15

| Standard deviations of 12-month percentage changes, 2000-15 ||||
|---|---|---|---|
| 10-yr Treasury Bond Price | 10-15-yr BB+ Bond Price | USD Major Currency Index | S&P 500 Equity Index |
| 6.0 | 9.8 | 8.2 | 18.1 |

*Sources:* Haver Analytics and author's calculations.

---

50 The Bank of England's QE purchases are placed off-balance sheet. Profits and losses flow directly to the UK Treasury. It is too soon to expect a substantial contribution to Eurosystem central bank profits from the large-scale QE begun in 2015.

Many observers have argued that the risk of losses on long-term bonds held by central banks gives QE a fiscal dimension that is different from conventional monetary policy.[51] The Bank of England, in particular, obtained approval from the government to put its QE purchases on the books of HM Treasury. However, in many countries central banks have long held large amounts of foreign exchange, which is roughly as risky as long-term bonds (Table 3.3). Moreover, as discussed below, it is the consolidated balance sheet of the government, including the central bank, which matters for public policy, not the balance sheet of the central bank alone.

Equities are generally riskier than bonds and foreign exchange (Table 3.3). However, a QE programme that purposely buys bonds with yields near zero is not likely to make much money in the long run. In contrast, buying equities in a recession could well have plenty of upside potential. One year after its equity purchases in August 1998, the value of the HKMA's equity holdings had risen 77% (not counting dividends). If the Fed had purchased the S&P 500 index in March 2009, at the launch of the main part of QE1, it would have enjoyed a total return of nearly 200% by year-end 2015 (assuming dividends were reinvested), or an annualised return of 25% for nearly five years running.

QE raises the probability of a central bank having a negative net worth at some point. Some observers have warned that the risk of future losses posed by large balance sheets may constrain monetary policy (Goodfriend, 2014). However, some central banks (for example, the Central Bank of Chile and the Czech National Bank ) have had extended periods with negative net worth and no apparent diminution of their policy effectiveness. Central banks cannot be insolvent as they are always free to issue liabilities to pay their expenses. As a rule, profit maximisation is not an objective of the central bank. However, losses at the central bank could become a serious political issue that might threaten central bank independence.

In the context of the consolidated government balance sheet, QE in government bonds does not change outstanding consolidated debt. It merely changes its composition from longer-term debt to short-term central bank reserves. This change in composition does not raise any fiscal risk *per se*.[52] QE (and negative policy rates) moreover reduce the long-run burden of public debt both by lowering the borrowing cost of the government and by supporting higher economic activity and tax revenues. These benefits will outweigh the potential for losses on the central bank's portfolio of assets in any plausible scenario. Furthermore, stabilising economic activity has broader social benefits than just increasing tax revenues.

---

51 A related issue is the potential conflict between central banks and finance ministries in terms of debt management. A central bank buying long-term bonds to reduce the term premium might find its actions offset by a finance ministry lengthening the maturity of its debt to take advantage of the lower term premium. Communication to avoid such a conflict is important.
52 To the extent that QE is conducted in private or foreign assets, it could increase consolidated debt, but only in extreme scenarios.

**Figure 3.13** Profitability of major central banks

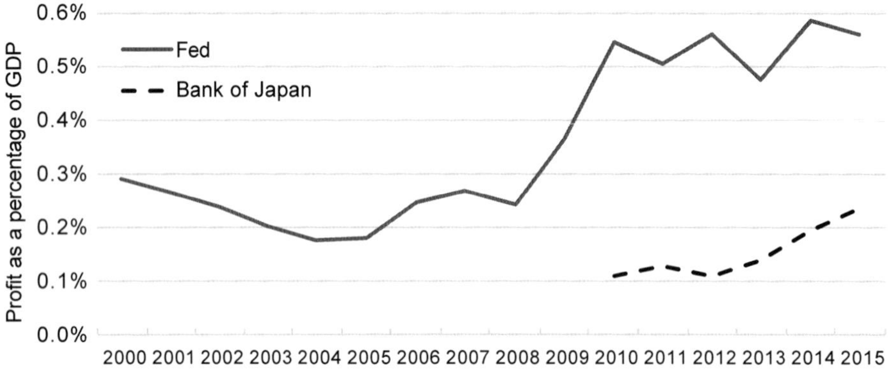

*Note:* Bank of Japan data not available prior to 2010. Profitability measures for the Fed and Bank of Japan are net income and operating profits excluding foreign exchange rate gains and losses, respectively.

## 3.3 Helicopter money

Whereas QE works like standard monetary policy by influencing the cost of finance, helicopter money policies seek to channel liquid purchasing power directly to agents more likely to spend it. Helicopter money thus combines QE with a strong fiscal component, and is therefore a tool that falls outside the mandate of most central banks. The coordinated fiscal monetary nature of helicopter money makes it a potentially very powerful policy package, however, and hence we briefly consider it here.

*How would helicopter money work?*

Because many households are cash- or liquidity-constrained,[53] they would be likely to spend much of any funds they received through a helicopter money mail-shot. Other forms of government outlay could have similar effects if accompanied by accommodating monetary action (QE) to prevent the increase in bond yields that would otherwise occur.[54]

On the other hand, market expectations of a subsequent future tightening of monetary policy would tend to weaken the aggregate demand impact of a helicopter money measure. After all, no central bank can convincingly pre-commit to never mopping up the base money created by the helicopter. Indeed, the *long-run* effect of HM on aggregate demand can under certain conditions be shown to be equivalent to that of a bond-financed deficit.[55]

---

53 Including those who have liquid assets but only sufficient to meet their precautionary savings or buffer-stock motives.
54 Note that heavily indebted governments face a more steeply upward-sloping cost of funds if default risk premium increases with debt ratios.
55 For example, sooner or later a central bank policy normalisation, requiring higher interest rates to mop-up excess liquidity, could adversely affect the consolidated income statement of the central bank and government, leading to much the same net position as if the deficit had been simply bond-financed (cf. Borio et al., 2016; Buiter, 2014).

It is for its potential *short-term* boost to demand that helicopter money seems attractive. Helicopter money is not needed except when market imperfections have resulted in the macroeconomy being stuck out of equilibrium with aggregate demand too low. By injecting liquidity where it can immediately unblock spending by liquidity-constrained economic agents, the net impact of helicopter money on spending in such conditions is unlikely to be fully offset by the influence of long-term expectations of future interest rate increases and the associated future tax burden (the incidence of which will in general be different).

The aim of helicopter money policies is not to increase the money base *per se*,[56] but to unleash spending by reducing actual or perceived constraints on doing so. As with all easing measures, the effectiveness of helicopter money could be dampened if poor communication around the policy announcement leads market participants to reassess risk upwards.

*Whose decision?*

Issues of legitimacy and governance need to be taken into account in determining the appropriate relative role of central bank and government in helicopter money.

Helicopter money could be conceivable as a 'central bank only' measure, taken by the central bank autonomously in pursuit of its mandate. But this would go beyond the normal scope of central banking. It is not so much that distributing spending power to households or other economic agents generates distributional effects – that is also true of standard monetary policy. Instead, what gives rise to concern is the fact that the distributional effects are not incidental or indirect side-effects of the policy, but directly impact on the chosen recipients (in contrast, for example, to an open market purchase, which has distributional effects on all market participants, not just on the counterparty of the trade). Under what mandate can the central bank decide how the spending power is to be distributed? The same cash amount for every citizen or resident? For every adult? For every household? Should the amount be related to household income, or to its income tax liability? Such questions clearly lie in the realm of government fiscal policy rather than central banking.[57]

Acknowledging the fiscal nature of the distribution of cash, helicopter money measures could be jointly agreed between the central bank and the government. But the independence of the central bank would be seriously compromised by having a joint decision on the monetary accommodation that would accompany the fiscal expansion. Indeed, the establishment of central bank independence was largely driven by the need to avoid a situation in which the central bank's policy was determined by fiscal needs and not by the goal of monetary or macroeconomic stability.

The central bank could preserve its independent approach by adapting its monetary policy actions to ensure delivery of its mandate, taking as given the policy actions of the fiscal authority. In that way, the central bank could safeguard monetary stability and ensure that exit from the helicopter money policy is not unduly deferred. But, in order to be confident that a fiscal expansion can safely

---

56  After all, the money base at present is a multiple of what it is likely to settle at (in nominal or real terms) when the disruption of current conditions has been resolved.

57  In the Eurozone, should the amount be the same for persons in different member states with substantially different average income levels? The amounts are not necessarily insignificant. If the current monthly QE volume being purchased by the ECB were instead allocated equally across the population of the Eurozone, the increase in annual personal income would amount to well over 25% in the lower-income countries such as Latvia, Lithuania and Slovakia.

be engineered, the fiscal authority will need to be aware of the likely response of the monetary authority to an expanded deficit. Accordingly, helicopter money would emerge as the combination of independent measures taken by the fiscal and monetary authorities, each taking account of what the other is doing with a shared understanding of the conjunctural situation and the policy needs.

Helicopter money is thus best thought of as a combination of fiscal and monetary actions that unlocks spending by agents who are currently cash-constrained; ideally, it results from independent measures employed by the fiscal and monetary authorities, each taking account of what the other is doing.

## 3.4 Forward guidance

If further easing is needed when nominal interest rates are at their floor, can more be achieved by the central bank making promises about the future? Such promises could be about how long into the future interest rates will be kept at the floor, or about the shape, scale and duration of future non-standard policy measures. Forward guidance is about the future evolution of policy instruments or tools, as distinct from statements about targets.

Forward guidance is typically the first tool a central bank should use to ease monetary conditions after rates have fallen below zero. The scope for forward guidance depends critically on what financial market participants expect about policy going forward. The evidence suggests that central banks can usefully influence market expectations of the future policy rate over a two- or three-year horizon, but evidence for an effect over a longer horizon is weak. If market interest rates are close to, or below, zero on bonds with maturities of up to three years or more, the scope for forward guidance on the policy rate becomes limited.

Some guidance has been merely qualitative, for example indicating that rates will not be increased for a "considerable" or "extended" period. More specific forms include calendar-based guidance (for example, specifying a number of quarters during which the policy rates will remain unchanged) and state-contingent guidance (for example, indicating threshold rates for inflation and/or unemployment outside of which no increase in the policy rate will occur). Forecasts of policy rate movements over coming quarters have also been provided and can be considered a form of forward guidance.[58,59]

*Forecast or promise?*

Forward guidance can be intended as a *forecast* (throwing light on the central bank's expectations about macroeconomic conditions and its reaction function) or as a *commitment*.[60] By committing itself to maintaining lower policy rates in the future than it would normally choose to, when that time comes, the central bank can create the expectation of a temporarily higher inflation in the future, thereby further lowering real long-term interest rates. Such a commitment is especially helpful at the zero lower bound (Eggertsson and Woodford, 2003).

---

58 For example, the anonymous "dots" which show the policy rate forecast made for certain future quarters by each member of the Federal Open Market Committee.
59 Announcements about the rate and intended duration of QE purchases are another form of forward guidance.
60 The terms "Delphic" and "Odyssean" have been proposed by Campbell et al. (2012) for these two (forecast and commitment) respectively.

*Effectiveness*

Calibrated theoretical models suggest that forward guidance at the zero lower bound can have powerful effects (cf. Del Negro et al., 2012; Coenen and Warne, 2014). However, it is difficult for forward guidance to significantly reduce expectations of future policy rates below the optimal path suggested by inflation developments in the future, given the inflation target. Such a commitment is time inconsistent and arguably very difficult for a central bank to achieve (Filardo and Hofmann, 2014; Bank of Canada, 2015; Moessner et al., 2015). This problem of time-inconsistency limits the loosening a central bank can achieve through forward guidance. Most observers would agree with Friedman (2014) that forward guidance has been less powerful than asset purchase programmes, largely because of the limits to the scope for its credible usage.

Among the early users of this policy tool were the central banks of New Zealand (which began publishing interest rate projections in 1997), Norway and Sweden, which may have been somewhat influential in affecting market expectations and long-term rates (cf. Woodford, 2012; Moessner et al., 2015).

The partial pre-commitment embodied in more recent forward guidance announcements on policy rates by the Bank of Canada, Bank of Japan, the Federal Reserve, the Bank of England and the ECB in recent years also appears to have been often effective in lowering long-term rates. For example, US 10-year Treasury bond yields fell by as much as a quarter of a percentage point in August 2011 when the Fed announced that low levels of interest rates were warranted at least through mid-2013. The ECB's use of forward guidance in July 2013 is seen as having achieved its objective of flattening the Eurozone yield curve at a time when the US curve had significantly steepened (ECB, 2014).

All in all, the evidence suggests that forward guidance on interest rates can be an effective tool, but requires great care if the intended message is to be clearly understood and believed by market participants (cf. Hoffman and Filardo, 2014; Bank of Canada, 2015).

## 3.5 Beyond forward guidance: Committing to higher future inflation

One way of addressing the time-inconsistency problem in forward guidance is to announce a steeper target path for prices, either by announcing a higher inflation target or by announcing a temporary price level target (as proposed by Svensson, 2003). To gain credibility, it is important to announce a target change that can be justified within the central bank's mandate. Inflation targets higher than the current targets are more consistent with central bank mandates, given recent trends in real interest rates and the possibility of large economic shocks. Shifting to a price level target would allow a central bank to let inflation overshoot after a period in which prices fell below the target path. We discuss in Section 4 the advantages and drawbacks of a price level target relative to a higher inflation target in meeting the central bank's mandate.

Markets are likely to be sceptical of any announcement of a higher inflation target in the absence of supporting policy actions, especially when a central bank has had trouble meeting the existing targets. However, if the announced target change is considered to be the right policy option for achieving the central

bank's mandate in the longer term, and if the central bank is able to consistently communicate this (as discussed in Section 4), it is more likely to be credible. Announcing a new target that implies a higher level of future inflation can act as commitment device for forward guidance. Moreover, if the target change is combined with direct stimulus of demand through negative interest rates and aggressive QE, this may further strengthen beliefs that the central bank has shifted toward a more stimulative regime and is willing to take the necessary actions to get there.

In 2013, as part of a broader package of monetary policy measures, the Bank of Japan announced that it was aiming for a target inflation rate of 2% over the coming two years. As discussed in more detail in Box 3.3, the announcement is likely to have helped in the initial rise of actual and expected inflation in the aftermath of the announcement, but subsequent supporting measures may not have been sufficient to sustain the initial positive impact. Overall, it appears that concrete policy actions are critical for successfully raising the inflation target in the lower bound.

---

**Box 3.3**   Abenomics

In December 2012, Shinzo Abe was elected prime minister of Japan. One of Abe's prominent campaign pledges was to choose a new governor of the Bank of Japan who would buy more government bonds and raise inflation.[61] In April 2013, newly appointed Governor Haruhiko Kuroda announced that the Bank of Japan would aim for inflation of 2% in about two years. To support this goal, the Bank of Japan began massive purchases of long-term government bonds, along with small purchases of equities and real estate investment trusts.

Prior to 2013, core inflation had languished around or below −0.5% for several years (see Figure 3.14.) Kuroda's appointment marked a clear turning point for Japanese inflation. The initial rise in inflation was supported importantly by a sharp depreciation of the yen in late 2012 and early 2013, which in turn reflected the prospect of loose monetary policy. However, the effect of exchange rates on consumer prices takes no more than two or three quarters to be completed (Ihrig et al., 2006). The continuation of higher inflation in late 2014 and 2015 was mainly driven by domestic factors, including an uptick in wage settlements. The unemployment rate in Japan has fallen steadily since Abe's election and is now at a 20-year low.

Long-term inflation expectations also rose after Abe's election. Professional forecasters' projections of consumer price inflation six to ten years ahead rose from 0.8% in October 2012 to 1.7% in April 2014 (Figure 3.14). There are relatively few inflation-indexed bonds in Japan and the market for them is not liquid; implied inflation compensation in bonds of long maturities nevertheless rose noticeably in 2013 (Bank of Japan, 2016, Chart 39).

---

61  "Abe pledges to make Bank of Japan buy bonds", *The Japan Times*, 19 November 2012.

**Box 3.3** (contd.)

There is no plausible explanation for the fall in unemployment and the rise in inflation and inflation expectations besides loose Japanese monetary policy. Although Abe did secure a modest fiscal stimulus in 2013, he instituted a significant rise in the consumption tax in April 2014. According to the OECD, Japan's underlying primary fiscal deficit contracted about 2 percentage points of GDP in the years 2014 and 2015 (OECD, 2016, p. 43). Japan's external environment has been roughly neutral; the benefit of low commodity prices has been offset by slower growth in many of Japan's main trading partners. Net exports made a negligible contribution to real GDP growth over the years 2013 to 2015.

Core inflation plateaued in 2014, probably a result of the contractionary effect of the consumption tax increase. In late 2014, the Bank of Japan increased the pace of bond purchases and inflation resumed its upward trend.

A second pause in the path of inflation occurred in late 2015. Governor Kuroda told reporters that the Bank of Japan would not adopt negative interest rates in December 2015.[62] Yet, in January 2016, the Bank of Japan surprised the markets with a small cut in its marginal deposit rate from 0.1% to –0.1%.[63] This was a small adjustment to the policy stance, and the political controversy it generated appears to have convinced markets that further cuts are not likely. Nominal bond yields have dropped substantially, especially for very long maturities, but yields on the few inflation-linked bonds of long maturity that exist have moved much less, suggesting an unwelcome fall in long-term inflation compensation. Figure 3.14 shows that core inflation and long-term survey expectations of inflation have slid down over the past six months.

Unless the Bank of Japan takes strong action, such as a substantial reduction in its deposit rate or a large-scale increase in equity purchases, it risks losing credibility. Falling expectations of long-term inflation would make it hard to raise actual inflation to the Bank of Japan's target.

Overall, the Japanese experience of the past three years demonstrates both the promise and the pitfalls of a combined programme of QE and raising inflation expectations.[64] It is not possible to disentangle the effects of the two components of this programme. However, it is clear that a promise to raise inflation without other policy actions to support this promise will not work. Indeed, a central bank must be willing to do whatever it takes in terms of lower interest rates and more QE to achieve its promise or it risks losing credibility and making its task much harder.

---

62 "Bank of Japan Kuroda says no need to adopt negative deposit rates in Japan", Reuters, 7 December 2015.
63 As mentioned previously, the majority of bank deposits at the Bank of Japan continue to receive interest at 0.1%.
64 De Michelis and Iaccoviello (2016) also argue that the Bank of Japan has boosted inflation but that "further measures are needed to raise inflation to 2%".

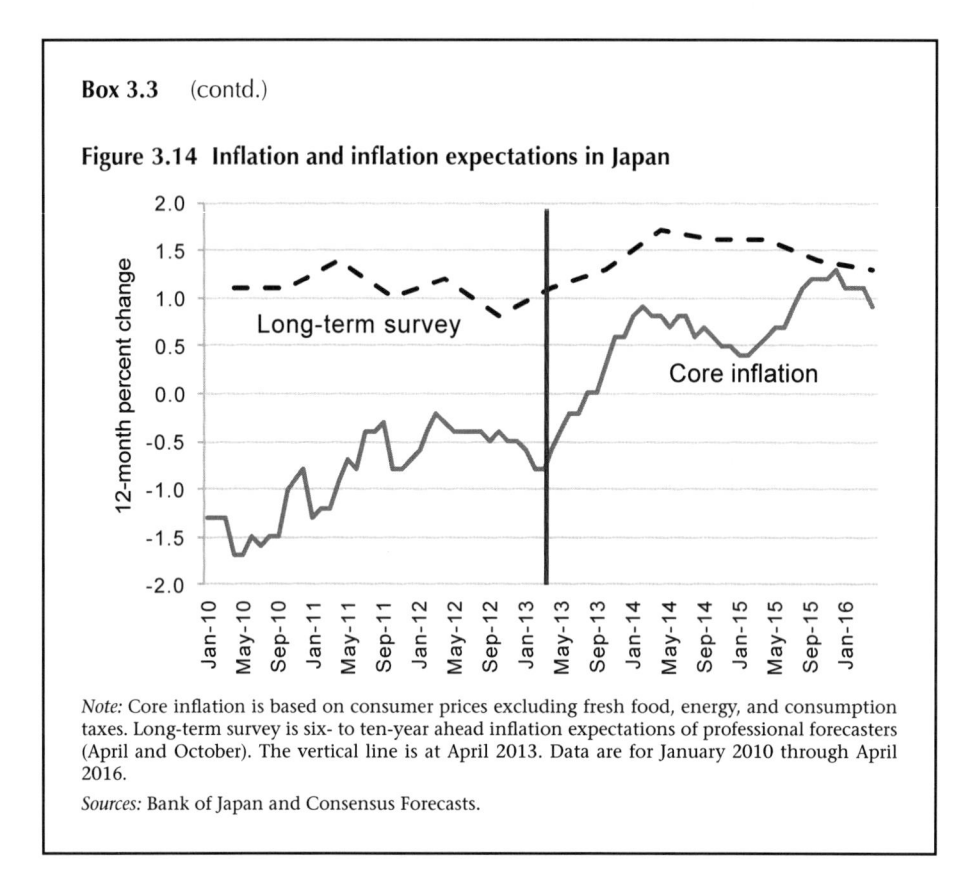

> **Box 3.3** (contd.)
>
> **Figure 3.14 Inflation and inflation expectations in Japan**
>
> *Note:* Core inflation is based on consumer prices excluding fresh food, energy, and consumption taxes. Long-term survey is six- to ten-year ahead inflation expectations of professional forecasters (April and October). The vertical line is at April 2013. Data are for January 2010 through April 2016.
>
> *Sources:* Bank of Japan and Consensus Forecasts.

## 3.6 Policy mix, interactions and financial stability

### 3.6.1 Policy mix

The best mix of policies to escape the lower bound constraint depends on the monetary and financial market characteristics and social preferences of a country – there is no one-size-fits-all. Some countries do not have the necessary domestic asset market depth for QE via securities purchases. In other countries, the transmission of negative interest rates may be hampered by banking sector frictions. Finally, the prospects for using forward guidance to affect inflation expectations depend on preferences and the institutional/political circumstances for committing to temporarily or permanently higher future inflation.

### 3.6.2 Policy interactions

Negative interest rates and QE interact in ways that are important to take into account when designing and implementing these measures. As discussed in Section 3.1, banks may not be able to pass on negative policy rates to retail deposits. If retail deposits constitute a large share of bank liabilities, then cutting interest rates below zero when deposits at the central bank constitute a significant proportion of the assets banks hold may constitute a shock to the profitability of

banks that could destabilise the banking sector. This was the reason the SNB and the Bank of Japan announced new tiering systems for the interest rates on central bank deposits at the same time they cut interest rates into negative territory. Tiering systems exempt large parts of the banks' deposits held with the central bank from the negative deposit rate.

QE is the main reason banks hold so many deposits at central banks. If interest rates are cut below zero before QE is implemented, and banks' holdings of central bank deposits are low, then there is little direct initial impact from the negative rate on bank profits. Subsequent QE purchases will tend to increase asset prices, including the prices of assets held by banks. Non-retail deposit funding cost will fall. In this case, a tiering system for central bank reserves may be less important, at least initially.

Cecchetti and Schoenholz (2016) argue for sequencing negative interest rates before QE for these reasons, but it may also be acceptable to embark on the two types of policies simultaneously. One argument for embarking on the two policies simultaneously is that central banks may wish to provide stimulus rapidly and yet they may wish to move slowly in cutting policy rates in order to guard against any large-scale switch to cash.

The fact that profitability in the banking sectors of negative interest rate countries has been strong suggests that tiering systems may not be necessary even with initially high levels of central bank reserves. Tiering systems moreover are hard to design in a way that distributes the implicit subsidy inherent in such systems fairly across different types of bank business models. As an alternative, central banks might try to coordinate a simultaneous transmission of negative rates to retail deposits, thereby restoring banks' net interest margin. To do this, central banks would have to accept the potential political cost of a likely unpopular policy.

### 3.6.3 Monetary accommodation and financial stability

By lowering risk-free interest rates, expansionary monetary policy encourages investors to buy other assets, raising the prices of those assets and reducing risk premiums. Of course, that is exactly the intention of the policy. It may become a dilemma for a central bank, however, if risk taking is accompanied by increasing leverage in the financial system or if the financial and business cycles are not in sync. Bank-credit-fuelled property price bubbles have been particularly troublesome (Schularick and Taylor, 2012). The worst-case scenario would be for an unsustainable leveraged asset bubble to grow while inflation and employment are trending downwards.

The long-standing debate as to whether monetary policy has any role to play in safeguarding financial stability continues. There is broad agreement that monetary policy is better suited to achieving stable prices and employment than to regulating leverage and financial exuberance. Much effort has gone into developing and implementing macroprudential measures such as higher general capital standards, countercyclical capital surcharges, restrictions on loan-to-value and borrower debt-to-income ratios, and many others. The question remains whether feasible macroprudential measures are sufficient to safeguard financial stability, and, if not, whether monetary policy should trade off a quantum of

macroeconomic stability in order to safeguard financial stability. We are sceptical of claims that monetary tightening in a recession can improve financial stability, but it is beyond the scope of this report to settle the debate.

We note that systemic financial stability concerns associated with easy monetary policy (low real interest rates) apply equally to standard monetary policy, QE, negative rates and forward guidance.[65] In the deflationary or recessionary environment in which economies are likely to be confronted with the lower bound on interest rates, financial risk taking tends to be too low relative to what is considered optimal. In such a world, the spillovers of monetary policy easing on financial stability are less negative than in the case of a robustly growing economy (Ubide, 2016). It is also important to recognise that economic stability has direct benefits for financial stability, so that easy monetary policy in a recession does not obviously raise financial risks on balance (Chodorow-Reich, 2014; Bernanke, 2015).

While not necessarily conclusive, an interesting study by Svensson (2016) calibrates the costs and benefits of adding a financial stability element to a monetary policy rule and finds that the economic costs far outweigh the benefits, even when macroprudential measures are judged insufficient by themselves to prevent a financial crash (see also Assenmacher-Wesche and Gerlach, 2010).

Relative to negative rates or higher target inflation, QE increases central bank control of financial assets. QE may increase perceptions of a limited downside to asset prices, given that the central bank is operating through them.[66] The central bank may need to communicate its intentions clearly.

---

[65] The monetary–financial trade-off can be affected by the specific nominal level of interest rates to the extent that there is money illusion or that financial institutions have nominal return targets. These cases are discussed in Section 3.1. We focus on the general case here.

[66] For example, many participants in the newly issued MBS market believed that the Fed had some target for MBS yields in 2009, when in fact Fed purchases were fixed in terms of quantity not price.

# 4 Raising the inflation target

Given the challenges and limits involved with using unconventional monetary policy at the lower bound, preemptive measures that would reduce the frequency of these challenges should be considered. The inflation target that central banks aim for when setting monetary policy is of central importance to the problem of the liquidity trap.

Countries should periodically reconsider their inflation target in light of expected future real interest rates and the amplitude of shocks that are likely to hit the economy. Already mentioned above is the potential use of such a revision to speed the escape from an existing liquidity trap, but there is also a case for raising the target in order to reduce the frequency of future liquidity trap events. The numerical level or range for inflation is usually not pre-set in legislation; it is generally left to the central bank to translate its legislative mandate into measurable goals or objectives.[67]

In advanced economies there has been considerable convergence towards a goal of about 2%, but this may reflect something of an historical accident. A clustering effect may have been operating, as each central bank looked over its shoulder at what its peers were deciding before settling on a rate. Indeed, the Riksbank explicitly stated that one reason for it having chosen 2% as the goal in 1993 was that "this was in line with the inflation targets in other industrial nations."

The optimal choice of target is not necessarily set in stone, and should be re-evaluated rationally based on consideration of the benefits and costs of a higher target. In particular, even if 2% was an appropriate target based on the conditions of the 1990s, both the prolonged liquidity trap since 2008 and the evidence of a secular fall in the neutral real interest rate argue for some upward revision. The transition to a higher inflation target may involve some disturbance. If done carefully and with the right supporting measures, however, these costs are unlikely to outweigh the benefits of having more monetary firepower in the long term.

What is needed is a credible, institutionalised review process for selecting the level of the inflation target. This should periodically re-evaluate the trade-off between the cost of a slightly higher average inflation rate and the benefit of reducing the risk of severe deflations or recessions. The selection, following such a process, of a higher inflation target should not threaten the credibility of the central bank's commitment to a stable macroeconomic regime. Instead, it could strengthen credibility inasmuch as it would improve the ability of the central bank to meet its mandate.

---

[67] Earlier proponents of raising inflation targets to reduce the risk of the liquidity trap include Posen (1998), Krugman (1998), Bernanke (2000) and Blanchard et al. (2010).

## 4.1 Benefits of raising the inflation target

Section 3.3 discusses the announcement of an inflation target as a possible tool for boosting an economy out of a liquidity trap. Here, we examine the long-run effect of a higher target on the frequency and severity of zero bound episodes.

Recall the Fisher equation: $i = r + \pi^e$. Raising the inflation target would raise the normal level of actual and expected inflation, and hence the normal level of the nominal interest rate. For example, if the long-run real interest rate is 1%, raising the inflation target from 2% to 4% would raise the long-run level of the nominal interest rate from 3% to 5%. Starting from this long-run level, the central bank would have an extra 200 basis points of conventional monetary easing available before the nominal rate hits zero. Policymakers would be better able to offset recessionary shocks and speed the return to full employment. We get quantitative estimates of the benefits of a higher inflation target from simulations of our simple macroeconomic model, presented in Box 4.1.

Moving inflation higher can have other benefits, apart from the avoidance of the liquidity trap, notably by easing (or 'greasing') the functioning of labour markets when there is downward wage rigidity. Even in the absence of a lower bound problem, researchers have found that unemployment in the United States and Europe is minimised with inflation rates in the range around and somewhat above 2% (Akerlof et al., 1996; Wyplosz, 2001). The tendency of standard price indexes to overestimate inflation, not least because of the difficulty of taking full account of the impact of new goods and quality improvements, also needs to be borne in mind as a reason for aiming at measured inflation above zero.

---

**Box 4.1**  The simulation with a higher inflation target

Figure 4.1 revisits our analysis of the Great Recession, examining how this experience might have been different if it occurred in a regime with a 4% rather than a 2% inflation target. Specifically, we assume the same behaviour of real variables through 2008Q3 as actually occurred, but assume that inflation and the nominal interest rate were 2 percentage points above their historical levels, and that 4% is the inflation target: $\pi^*$ in the Taylor rule. To isolate the effects of a higher target, we do not allow the nominal interest rate to fall below the slightly positive levels actually observed over 2009-2015. The figure compares outcomes during the Great Recession under this scenario to actual history.

Even under our assumption of higher initial inflation and nominal rates, the demand shocks of the Great Recession quickly push the economy to the zero bound. The good news is that, with higher inflation, a zero nominal rate implies a highly negative real rate, which accelerates the recovery of employment. We find that unemployment outcomes with a 4% target would have been substantially better than actual outcomes and that the improvement is essentially the same as the improvement in the simulation with a lower bound of –2% (Figure 3.8). The average unemployment gap from 2010 through 2015 is about 0.7 percentage points lower than in the historical data.

**Box 4.1** (contd.)

**Figure 4.1** Great Recession with and without higher inflation target

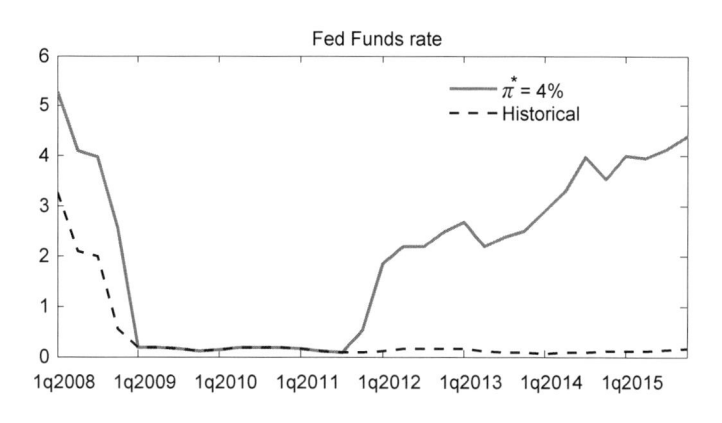

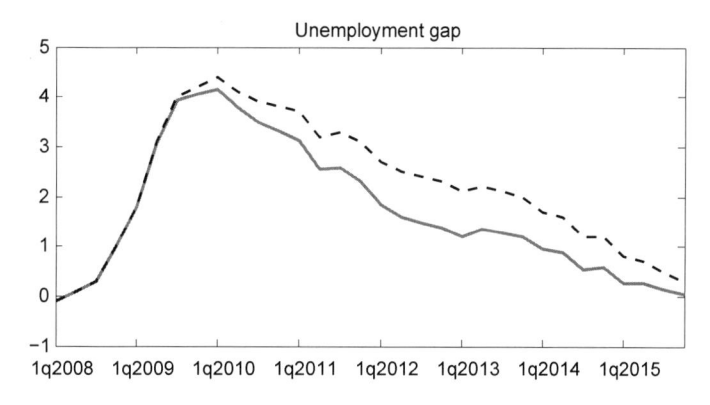

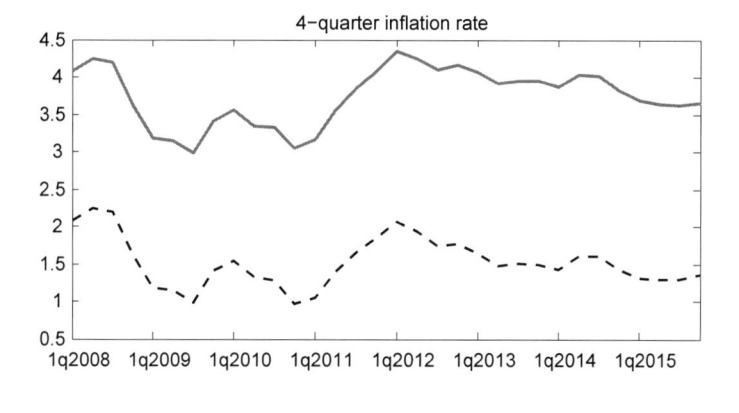

## 4.2 Costs of a higher inflation target

Would raising the inflation target by a percentage point or two have major costs, compared to the benefits of mitigating episodes of underemployment? If we accept that the neutral level of real interest rates has been falling for many years, and that monetary policy needs to be prepared to cope with shocks on a larger scale than was envisaged during the years of the Great Moderation, it is not hard to argue that there may have been an increase in the optimum target rate of inflation by one or two percentage points.

To counter such an assertion, it would be necessary to claim either that an increase of that order in the average rate of inflation would have sizable other adverse microeconomic or macroeconomic effects, or that an increase in the target would lead to costly variability in the inflation rate around its average level.

### 4.2.1 Costs of modestly higher average inflation

To be set against the gains from avoidance of liquidity trap problems are the social costs of various microeconomic distortions that may be associated with having a higher average rate of inflation. These costs, well aired in policy discussions over the years,[68] include the 'shoe leather' costs of economising on cash holdings and a potentially related overinvestment in the financial system; distortions from the interaction between an unindexed tax system and inflation; and greater variability of relative prices resulting from 'menu costs' of frequent price adjustment. Quantifying these costs is a task which has engaged many scholars, using different approaches, and without much convergence of opinion.

Some of the costs of inflation may be drifting lower than in the past. Take shoe leather costs. These are usually measured by the area under the demand curve for non-interest bearing money (M1) expressed as a function of the nominal rate of interest.[69] But, likely thanks to technological changes, the demand for M1 has shifted in and steepened, lowering that area (even at 5%, the estimates for the United States in Ireland (2009) imply a welfare loss from this source of less than 0.075% of GDP).

Potentially significant economic efficiency losses are also implied by the staggered nominal price-setting assumed in much recent theory (e.g. Woodford, 2003; Gali, 2008) because it results in a dispersion in relative prices across firms, which in turn leads to a misallocation of productive resources. But, based on recent research findings, it is not clear that higher inflation implies more relative dispersion. For example, using micro data on US consumer prices, Nakamura et al. (2016) find that the level of price dispersion has not varied with the level of inflation (even in the 1970s, when inflation rose to double digits), likely because higher inflation has led firms to adjust their nominal prices more frequently, and this offsets the effect on dispersion arising from staggered price setting.

---

68  See, for example, the literature review prepared by ECB staff to underpin its latest formal assessment of monetary policy strategy (Rodríguez-Palenzuela et al., 2003). An earlier literature explores a wide range of impacts of different inflation rates in an economy dominated by nominal contracts, for example on the market value of equities and on the incidence of corporate default (e.g. Modigliani and Cohn, 1979; Wadhwani, 1986).

69  Ironically for the context of our report, the well-known basic Friedman rule for monetary policy, derived simply by minimising these shoe leather costs, calls for a constant zero nominal interest rate – but for negative average inflation!

The importance of costs, such as those arising from the interaction of inflation and an unindexed system of taxation which could be non-negligible at even low rates of inflation (Feldstein, 1997), may also vary over time depending on the level and structure of taxation.[70]

Higher inflation may make long-term financial planning more difficult. For example, the nominal level of wealth needed for retirement in 30 years is considerably larger with 4% than with 2% inflation. That can complicate planning about saving and asset allocation, because it takes effort and sophistication to convert nominal to real magnitudes. And it has to be acknowledged that a higher inflation target would move us farther from the definition of price stability given by Greenspan (2001) (while eschewing the idea of a precise inflation target), namely an environment in which inflation is low enough that "it does not materially enter into the decisions of households and firms".

However, to our knowledge, nobody has sought to measure the magnitude of welfare losses from inflation through this channel. We cannot prove that the cost is small, but it seems modest compared to the benefits of a higher inflation target. We have argued that a higher inflation target would mitigate episodes of elevated unemployment rates, which can be disastrous for people's economics plans. We invite the reader to consider what would make your retirement planning more difficult: learning that your central bank's inflation target is rising from 2% to 4%, or learning that you have an increased risk of losing your job?

Turning to the macro level, many scholars have shown a cross-country correlation between high inflation and weaker national economic growth. Yet few if any of these studies indicate any significant benefits for growth of pushing inflation rates below about 5% or so.

Our sense that a modest increase in the average inflation rate from about 2% would not add markedly to efficiency or growth penalties receives some reinforcement from considering trends in public attitudes to inflation in the mid- to-late 1980s when, after surging into double digits in the 1970s, inflation was stabilised in many advanced economies at around 4%.[71]

Central bankers' success – spearheaded by Paul Volcker – in reducing inflation to 4% is often called the 'conquest' of inflation (e.g. Sargent, 1999). Policymakers appeared satisfied at that time to live with 4% inflation. In the United States, the Fed did not tighten policy to control inflation until the end of 1988, when inflation started to rise above 4% (Romer and Romer, 1994).

The general public also appeared satisfied with 4% inflation. Reporting that, from 1972 to 1982, Gallup polls found that the percentage of the US population that considered inflation "the most serious problem facing the nation" ranged from 30% to 80%, and that this percentage was highly correlated with the inflation rate, Fischer (1996) remarks that "the concern about inflation disappeared rapidly once inflation dropped below 5%; inflation has not been a serious issue in the polls since 1986". According to Google books, mention of "inflation" in English-, French- or German-language books fell back sharply from its peak intensity in the late 1970s or early 1980s, also suggesting that the problem was no longer

---

70  Indeed, the seigniorage revenue associated with inflation rate facilitates a reduction in other distorting taxes for a given revenue target, thereby partly offsetting the distorting interaction between inflation and a given set of tax rates.
71  Average annual CPI inflation 1984-89 in the United States was 3.7%, in France it was 3.9% and in the United Kingdom it was 4.6%  (rates in Germany and Japan were much lower.)

attracting public attention by the mid-1980s. All in all, if we look back at the period of 4% inflation, it is hard to see any signs that the economy suffered significant damage from inflation running fairly steadily at that rate.

### 4.2.2 Inflation variability

Policymakers often emphasise not the level of inflation per se, but the effect of a higher inflation target on inflation variability and uncertainty. If a central bank maintained a firm commitment to a 4% target, would inflation vary around this target by more than around a 2% target? A large empirical literature documents that the mean and variance of the inflation rate are correlated across countries and time periods. This fact is important because more variable inflation has undesirable effects such as arbitrary redistributions of wealth and greater risk in nominal contracts. It could also have a chilling effect on long-term investment planning (Huizinga, 1993).

There is no reason, however, that a higher inflation target must raise inflation variability if the target is stable. The historical correlation between the mean and variance of inflation reflects the fact that periods of high average inflation have also been times in which inflation is not anchored. In the 1970s, policymakers sometimes let inflation drift up by accommodating supply shocks, and sometimes decided to tighten policy to disinflate. We have seen relatively stable inflation with a 2% target because policy has sought to meet the target. Advanced economies have not seen sustained periods in which policymakers sought to stabilise inflation at a level significantly above 2%.

In principle, there might be some feature of the economy that inevitably causes inflation control to be less accurate with a higher target. But Stock and Watson (2007, 2015) provide evidence to the contrary. Their work distinguishes between short-run volatility arising from temporary shocks to inflation and long-run volatility arising from changes in trend inflation. The unconditional variance of inflation depends on both types of volatility. Historically, a higher level of inflation has increased long-run volatility, but this effect could be eliminated by commitment to a target. Historically, higher inflation has not been associated with a greater variance of temporary shocks to inflation. The variance of temporary shocks has been quite steady over the last 50 years, even as the economy has experienced periods of high average inflation, like the 1970s, and low average inflation, like today. If average inflation becomes anchored at 4%, so that temporary shocks are the only source of inflation variability, we should not expect higher variability than we see with a 2% anchor.

Indeed, there are reasons to believe that raising the inflation target modestly would *reduce* inflation uncertainty compared to the 2% regime of today. The reason is that, as stressed throughout this report, a 2% target means the economy spends substantial time at the zero bound on interest rates. This situation creates uncertainty about the central bank's ability to control inflation, and about the effects of unconventional policy tools.

Consistent with this idea, the period since 2008 has generally been one of a low level of inflation but high uncertainty about future inflation. Indicators of inflation uncertainty increased across countries in the aftermath of the crisis, as documented by Gerlach et al. (2011). Kitsul and Wright (2013) infer probability distributions for future US inflation from the prices of various options tied to

the inflation rate. They find that despite the Federal Reserve's insistence that it will produce 2% inflation in the future, markets have considerable doubt, and ascribe a substantial probability to large target misses in both directions. In 2011, markets ascribed a probability approaching 10% to the average inflation rate over the next ten years being negative, and a 30% probability to it exceeding 4%.

It is not hard to understand why this uncertainty arises. On the one hand, at the zero bound there is doubt about a central bank's ability to ease policy further and avoid deflation if adverse shocks occur. At the same time, the huge expansion of the monetary base resulting from unconventional policies raises fears that inflation will rise more than desired if the economy recovers strongly. A higher inflation target would help move the economy away from the zero bound and return us to a regime in which central banks adjust short-term interest rates to offset both positive and negative shocks to inflation. In that regime, there is greater assurance that the central bank can control inflation over the medium run.

In the Eurozone too, there is considerable market uncertainty about future inflation. Interestingly, neither the degree of subjective uncertainty, the degree of disagreement between different forecasters nor the market risk premium for inflation uncertainty are consistently positively correlated with the current level of inflation (Garcia and Werner, 2010).

## 4.3  Credibility and the inflation target

So far, we have assumed that a central bank can choose to anchor inflation at a target above 2%. Perhaps the leading argument against an increase in the inflation target is that it would weaken commitment to any target, or at least weaken the public's belief in the target and therefore lead to an unmooring of inflation expectations.

Bernanke expressed this idea in 2012: "The Federal Reserve, over a long period of time, has established a great deal of credibility in terms of keeping inflation low, around 2%.... If we were to go to 4% and say we're going to 4%, we would risk a lot of that hard-won credibility, because folks would say, well, if we go to 4%, why not go to 6%? It'd be very difficult to tie down expectations at 4%" (Bernanke, 2012). Other central bankers have made similar statements.

The rationale for this concern is not clear. In other contexts, policymakers argue that a central bank should determine the optimal strategy for meeting its mandate, explain this strategy to the public, and carry it out. We have learned from recent experience that a 2% inflation target is too low for achieving a mandate for full employment, and also for price stability because deflation is a risk at the zero bound. The risk of credibility loss may in fact be higher if targets are not revised upward. In several countries currently, the difficulty of meeting inflation and unemployment goals has given rise to questions about central banks' ability and willingness to meet their mandates.

Central banks should seek to make credible their commitment to meeting their mandates – not their commitment to a particular and perhaps arbitrary level for the inflation target. Policymakers could explain that current targets are no longer consistent with the mandate, and that this lesson motivates an increase in the

target. They could also explain that this increase does not reflect a shift in the relative importance attached to inflation and unemployment, but rather new information about the trade-offs they face.

## 4.4 How to implement a new target

One strategy for achieving credibility would be to adopt a periodic review process for reconsidering the inflation target and other aspects of monetary policy. Such a process could be modelled on the current practice of the Bank of Canada, which reviews its inflation-targeting strategy every five years. The inflation target would not be changed frequently or 'opportunistically', but it would be re-evaluated in light of major developments such as the post-2008 liquidity trap.[72]

As it happens, the Bank of Canada's latest five-year policy review will be completed later in 2016. The Bank has announced that one major issue under consideration is an increase in its inflation target from the current range of 1% to 3%. Bank of Canada economists have been studying the issue for several years, and policymakers will make a decision based on "a careful analysis of the costs and benefits of adjusting the target" (Côté, 2014).

Shifting to a periodic review process for the level of the inflation target would also be relatively straightforward in practical terms. New analytical capacity and competencies to address the question of what is the optimal inflation target for the next inter-review period would need to be developed. Central bank communication around the target framework should be prepared. But other parts of the central banks' monetary policy operating framework would operate as usual. In this sense, moving to a higher inflation target is likely to require less change of current central bank practices and frameworks than do other proposals for target or mandate changes to address the lower bound problem (such as those considered below).

An increase in a central bank's inflation target might involve a transitional period of learning, in which inflation uncertainty is greater than usual. This is one reason why inflation target reviews should occur according to a predefined schedule and not be frequent. The uncertainty can moreover be minimised through good central bank communication. There is little reason to think that a transition to modestly higher inflation would cause significant harm to the economy. History does not suggest that it would be 'difficult to tie down expectations'. Inflation expectations, as measured by surveys, generally follow actual inflation with a lag. In the United States, for example, they have followed the rise of actual inflation in the 1960s and 1970s and the fall since then. If inflation rises to 4%, it seems unlikely that expectations will overshoot that level.

New Zealand has raised its inflation target twice since the inception of the policy in 1989. First, it widened the target band from 0–2% to 0–3% in 1996. Then it narrowed the band to 1–3% percent in 2002. The net effect was to raise the target midpoint from 1% to 2%. The reason for the increase was a general feeling that the original band was too restrictive. To some extent there may have been a confusion between the benefits of a higher target and allowing a greater role for an implicit objective on economic growth or employment. In any

---

[72] The Bank of England's inflation target is reviewed every year by the governor and the Chancellor of the Exchequer. Arguably, a longer period between reviews, such as Canada's five years, is better for careful assessment of policies and for avoiding opportunism.

event, there were not widespread concerns about an unmooring of expectations; inflation has averaged close to the new midpoint since 2002, and has recently drifted below target.

We have recently seen the experience of Japan in raising its inflation target to 2% from an implicitly lower level, as discussed in more detail in Box 3.3. This action has not led to an unmooring of expectations.

## 4.5 What about a price level target?

A number of economists have advocated an alternative to a higher inflation target as a strategy for avoiding liquidity traps: a price level target (e.g. Eggertsson and Woodford, 2003). Under this strategy, the central bank targets a path of the aggregate price level that grows at a fixed rate. This commitment means that, when inflation deviates from its average level, the central bank does not simply seek to return inflation to that level. Below-average or above-average inflation pushes the price level away from the targeted path, so the policy rule dictates that inflation must temporarily overshoot its average in the other direction to bring the price level back to its target path.[73]

The key difference between price-level targeting and inflation targeting as usually practiced is that inflation targeting ignores the past: the central bank targets future inflation without taking any account of whether recent inflation has undershot or overshot the target. In fact, though, inflation-targeting central banks such as the ECB have never explicitly made this distinction. Indeed, many statements by the ECB have emphasised its achievement in keeping the average Eurozone inflation rate close to 2% since the establishment of the currency. For the ECB to compensate a period of undershoot with a subsequent period of overshoot in order to keep average experienced inflation close to 2% would be consistent with the its formal mandate. A decision to interpret its target in that light could help it escape faster from the lower bound.

A disadvantage of moving to a price level target is that it might prove hard to explain that below-average inflation would be followed by above-average inflation and vice versa. The policy would work poorly if it were not fully understood and credible. This point was made by the Bank of Canada in 2011 when it considered but ultimately rejected the idea of adopting a price level target. Simulations by the Bank of Canada found that price-level targeting is effective at stabilising the economy under full credibility and fully rational expectations, but that it increases output volatility if inflation expectations are to some degree backward looking or anchored to the average inflation rate.

---

73 Not discussed here is nominal GDP targeting, an alternative goal or mandate aimed at improved stabilisation of the economy but not specifically designed to deal with the lower bound. To the extent that it is the level (rather than growth) of nominal GDP that is being targeted, this variant would have some of the attributes of price level targeting in the present context.

An alternative to choosing an internal goal such as inflation is to focus on an external anchor to achieve stability. [74] Exchange rate pegs represent a very conspicuous policy commitment device and are free of measurement error. However, they are vulnerable to speculation and, although some pegs have been maintained for many decades, historically most pegs have eventually been abandoned under the pressure of a loss of foreign exchange reserves, or the high interest rates – or both – needed to sustain them in the face of outflows. They are not practical options for the larger currencies.

---

74  Svensson's (2003) "Foolproof Way" to escape the liquidity trap combines a temporary price level target, announced in advance to be exited once the announced high path for prices is achieved, and combined with a devaluation and a crawling exchange rate peg that supports the credibility of the target. The proposal has a lot of merit as an alternative strategy to getting out of the liquidity trap. The main disadvantage, if not the only one, is that it would be difficult to communicate such a temporary change to monetary policy strategy. The exchange rate component of the "Foolproof Way" can be seen as beggar-thy-neighbour by some. However, raising the inflation target has a similar exchange rate effect. All successful monetary policy loosening should be expected to lead to a depreciation, as the future price level should be higher.

# 5 Monetary policy in a post-cash economy

If a country's payments system is fully electronic and no physical money circulates, then there is no asset with a fixed nominal value that will allow market participants to avoid a nominal negative interest rate. In that case, the normal instrument of monetary policy – the short-term policy rate – can in principle be cut as far below zero as a central bank deems necessary for achieving its mandate. For example, banks' deposit and lending rates can be set at highly negative levels. If individuals and institutions had the option to hold cash, this would likely produce a massive shift to cash and nobody would borrow or lend at the negative rates targeted by the central bank. That cannot happen, however, if cash does not exist. Rogoff (2014) notably argues for phasing out cash because a cashless monetary system is not subject to a lower bound on interest rates. His case is also based on, and perhaps better known for, the desire to reduce the costs to society associated with the use of cash for illegal purposes.

If monetary policy is not constrained by a lower bound in cashless economies, optimal inflation targets in such countries may be lower – perhaps even lower than current targets.

Phasing out cash is not a realistic policy option in the short term, but we believe that market-driven developments in payments systems make cashless societies inevitable in many countries in the longer term. This coming transformation in payments systems will not be unique in historical perspective. The nationalisation of money in the 17th century, the shift from gold to fiat currency in the 20th century (James, 2015), and the abolition of national currencies in European countries in 1999 were arguably even more profound. This does not mean that the transmission to cashless economies will be smooth or quick, however, as payment habits and public perceptions of the role of cash and negative interest rates may be very persistent.

We show below that some countries are particularly far ahead when it comes to the adoption of electronic payments systems. In such countries, phasing out cash in a socially responsible way could be within reach, and could soon address the problem of the lower bound on interest rates. We subsequently discuss monetary policy in cashless economies, and touch on other policy aspects of current trends in the use of cash as well as the transition toward a post-cash economy.

## 5.1 Markets are driving payments systems away from cash

Current market-driven developments in electronic payments systems are reducing the use of cash in most countries and will continue to do so in the coming decades. The use of card payments as a substitute for cash has been increasing for many years.[75] In the past five years, the shift toward cashless payments has accelerated as mobile contactless payments systems are gaining ground quickly in some countries.

The developments in electronic payments differ strongly across countries, however.[76] Figure 5.1 shows that outstanding cash as a percentage of GDP has remained stable in the Scandinavian countries, Australia, Canada and the UK since the turn of the century. Sweden has seen an outright decline in outstanding cash, from 4% of GDP in 2000 to below 2% in 2015.

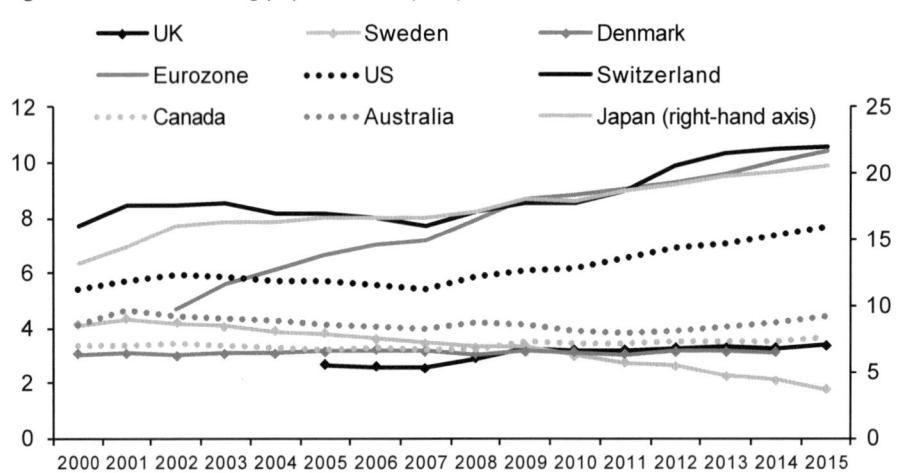

**Figure 5.1** Outstanding paper currency in percent of GDP.

*Sources:* National central banks.

In contrast, outstanding amounts of cash have increased in Switzerland, the United States, and the Eurozone.[77] The growth in outstanding cash in some countries is likely to reflect factors that are not related to the use of cash in retail payments, however, such as cash hoarding at low interest rates, flight to safety into the main international currencies, and demand for cash from illegal

---

[75] In Denmark, the ratio of cash-settled transactions in total retail transactions fell from 80% in 1991 to 26% in 2011. These numbers are estimated as the share of turnover in retail transactions which cannot be accounted for by electronic payments. It is likely to have fallen further in the past five years as the use of new mobile-technology-based electronic payment instruments has sharply increased. In Sweden, 20% of retail transactions were in cash in 2014. In comparison, 33% of the value of retail transactions is estimated to have been in cash and cheques in the United States in 2013, and estimates for the Eurozone as a whole tend to be above 50%, with strong variation among the member countries (ECB, 2011; Betalingsraadet, 2013; Bennet et al. 2014; Bean et al. 2015; also Danmarks Nationalbank payment statistics for 2015).

[76] See also Humphrey (2010) for an overview of differences in retail payments systems across countries and institutional/historical explanations of these.

[77] Bagnall et al. (2014) find important heterogeneity in the use of cash in retail transactions across a different but overlapping sample of countries, based on survey data.

transaction purposes (Rogoff, 2014; Sands, 2016).[78] In fact, electronic means of payment are gaining ground in countries where outstanding cash is growing. Figure 5.2 shows that currency in circulation is inversely related to the use of electronic card payment across a number of countries. The increases in card payments since 2000 were especially strong in Australia, Canada, Denmark, Sweden, the United States and the United Kingdom, whereas increases in electronic payments were less notable in Switzerland, Japan and the Eurozone.

**Figure 5.2**  Number of card payment per capita and physical currency in circulation, 2013

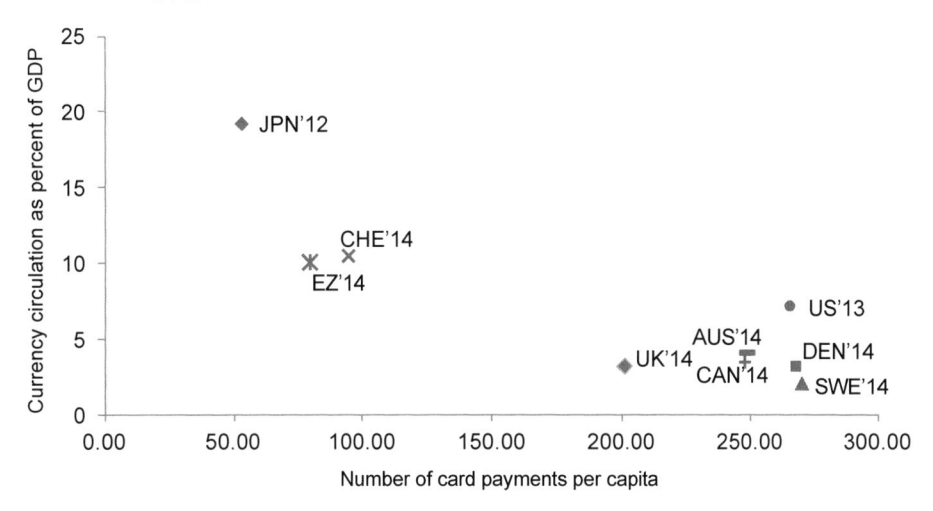

*Sources:* ECB, BIS (CGFS), national central banks.

National surveys of the means of payments in retail transactions confirm a decline in the use of cash relative to electronic means of payment across countries, including those that have seen their outstanding cash increase.

The adoption of electronic payments systems is likely to continue to accelerate in coming years, and the role of cash in payments systems will keep declining.[79] More and more services are provided online, without point of sale (POS) access. The use of smartphones with access to mobile means of payment is increasing. The fintec (financial technology) industry competes to innovate for these new markets.[80] The cost of electronic means of payment is hence likely to continue to fall. Once a cheap, broadly accepted and convenient electronic means of payment is adopted, cash will tend to be used less, because it is neither cheap nor convenient. Studies show that cash tends to be the most costly means of payment in retail payments, measured both in terms of the cost faced by the consumer and in terms of the cost to society as a whole. Most of us pay a fee to take out cash, and using it requires planning to hold the right amount of cash

---

78  If the use of cash for legal retail transactions purposes becomes insignificant in future, the only remaining reason for central banks to produce and supply cash would be to satisfy cash hoarding demand and demand due to illegal payments, which still would provide seigniorage revenues – a point also made in Rogoff (2014).
79  Wang and Wolman (2014) estimate that the use of cash in retail transactions in the United States is declining by an average of 2.5% per year.
80  See also Committee on Payments and Market Infrastructures (2015) on development of digital currencies.

in our wallets. Paying with cash at the point of sale takes longer and is more cumbersome than simply accepting an electronic payment on the smartphone, and we increasingly tend to choose the latter option even if we have cash in our wallet. The societal cost of cash additionally includes the cost – both pecuniary and environmental – of producing, maintaining, managing and destroying physical cash. Retail customers do not factor these costs into their means of payments decision as they are borne by the cash handling authorities.

Cash has the advantage that it still is more broadly accepted in retail payments than other means of payments in most countries, and a cash transaction is settled instantaneously so there is no settlement risk. But both of these factors may be changing. New mobile payments technologies are largely instantaneous, and are associated with such low costs that they are likely to become universally accepted by people with a mobile phone and a bank account.[81] This also makes intra-family and other private transfers – currently typically carried out in cash because card transactions require terminals – possible and instantaneous at the click of a smartphone. All this suggests that electronic and mobile payments are likely to become increasingly preferred to cash in the future. In this future, the role left for cash will be for hoarding and for conducting transactions intended to be kept private. As most counterparties will prefer electronic means of payment, this also suggests that large cash transactions will increasingly draw attention as being suspicious, whether the purpose of the transaction is legal or not.

## 5.2 Monetary policy without cash

It is not enough that cash be replaced by electronic money in the payments system to remove the lower bound on interest rates. As long as cash still exists, monetary policy will be subject to a lower bound. The convertibility of central bank reserves into cash would have to be fully suspended for monetary policy to become completely symmetric above and below zero. In most countries, a suspension of convertibility into cash would require legal action, and an unfavourable public opinion could delay such a step even if cash were no longer needed for payments. As discussed in Section 3.1, there is a lack of public acceptance and understanding of negative interest rates, partly rooted in money illusion, and this could lead some to want to hold on to cash as an insurance policy against central banks introducing negative interest rates. Perceptions and understanding may change over time, however, as experiences with negative policy rates evolve. Targeted central bank communication can play a role in this process.

Without cash, monetary policy can operate exactly the same way below zero as it currently operates in normal times above the lower bound. Central bank reserves would remain the anchor and numeraire currency, just as central bank reserves plus cash together constitute the numeraire currency today. Inflation targeting frameworks can remain intact, if these frameworks are considered appropriate for ensuring the mandate of price and macroeconomic stability today.

---

81 Examples are Mobile Pay in Denmark and Swish in Sweden.

The benefits and costs of a higher inflation target would change, however. While most of the benefits and costs listed in Section 4 would still apply, the benefits from higher inflation in the form of avoiding the lower bound constraint on monetary policy would fall away. To the extent that current low inflation targets have factored in a small but non-zero probability of hitting the lower bound, future inflation targets in cashless economies may in fact be even lower than current inflation targets. Adopting a recurrent review process for adjusting the inflation target to ensure that it remains consistent with the central bank mandate over time would accommodate such changes in future optimal inflation targets.

For some countries, actively accelerating the move toward a cashless economy could be a long-term strategy for preventing the incidence of the lower bound constraint on monetary policy. Phasing out cash in order to remove the effective lower bound is not a crisis option, however. It would involve far-reaching changes to money and payments systems and to the nature of money that are unrealistic at short notice. As long as society is not set up for cashless retail payments that are accessible for all population groups, cash will have a role to play. This suggests an interim period on the path toward a cashless payments system that will require other monetary policy tools to address episodes when the lower bound on interest rates binds. Temporarily raising the inflation target, as well as modestly negative interest rates and QE, are possible interim tools.

As an alternative interim solution, Buiter (2007, 2009) and Agarwal and Kimball (2015) propose decoupling the value of cash from electronic money, and letting cash and electronic money circulate as two separate currencies with a central bank-controlled exchange rate between them. This would allow the central bank to gradually devalue cash in terms of electronic money over time, thereby creating a negative yield on cash in terms of electronic money. Such a system would effectively remove the lower bound on interest rates but would preserve cash as a means of payment. Many unanswered questions remain, however, relating to how such a system would work. Notably, legal and structural changes would be required over which the central bank usually does not have authority.[82]

## 5.3 Other policy aspects of post-cash economies

Currently, objections to reducing the role of cash mainly reflect concerns unrelated to monetary policy. The need to possess a smartphone, or otherwise have access to the internet, to participate in the electronic payments systems that are emerging suggests a challenge for those parts of the population that are excluded from or do not wish to adopt the necessary new technologies. These challenges will increase as the parts of retail commerce that do not operate with cash increase.[83]

---

[82] One example is the question of legal tender. The legal framework governing financial contracts specifies in which tender financial contracts are honoured, and it will usually refer to domestic legal tender. With two domestic currencies circulating, there are two legal tenders with different values. Addressing this problem would require controversial legal reform.

[83] The growth in online retail is an important reason, but use of cash for other transactions is also likely to decline unless explicitly countered by legislation.

How should authorities ensure access to broadly accepted means of payment by all population segments in the face of increased use of electronic means of payment? Some countries are addressing this question with legislation that requires retail outlets to accept cash.[84] The problem remains, however, that online retail and new and strongly growing web-based business models cannot access cash payments. Authorities could alternatively implement policies that increase the rate of adoption of new and efficient payments technologies across all segments of the population.[85]

A related aspect of the declining use of cash is the issue of legal tender. Cash and central bank reserves are both legal tender, whereas other forms of money, including bank deposits, are not. If central banks are required to make legal tender available to all citizens and cash is disappearing, central banks can consider opening up access to central bank reserve accounts to all citizens.[86] Another option is to provide an electronic form of central bank cash (Kumhof and Barrdear, 2016) – a number of central banks are currently exploring options for electronic cash provision. Alternatively, certain types of bank deposits can be subjected to more stringent deposit insurance requirements or directly linked to central bank reserves, and thereby be made legal tender.

Another policy issue is that electronic means of payment are traceable, and hence do not ensure the privacy of citizens' transactions. This is an advantage in crime and terrorism prevention. If ensuring the privacy of legal transactions remains an important policy objective, however, there are ways to allow for privacy in electronic payments systems, with the trade-off that creating such anonymous systems facilitates illegal transactions.

If going cashless is a policy priority – for efficiency, legal, monetary policy or other reasons – the authorities can catalyse or coordinate the development of new payments systems, invest in the necessary technological infrastructure and thereby steer the direction these systems take.[87] Furthermore, central banks can provide electronic currency for the broader public (Kumhof and Barrdear, 2016). Apart from solving the problem of access to legal tender discussed above, this can broaden the access to electronic payments for all citizens, thereby increasing efficiency in payments through universality, and help accelerate the possible phasing out of cash.

In conclusion, the market-driven adoption of electronic payment systems is leading to some countries becoming all but cashless. There is no lower bound on interest rates in fully cashless economies, where monetary policy can operate symmetrically above as well as below zero. Going cashless would hence allow for greater macroeconomic stability, as well as lower inflation targets, than when monetary policy is at risk of being constrained by the lower bound.

The speed with which countries are becoming cashless, and whether or not it is a desirable public policy goal to become cashless, depends on how challenges of social inclusion in electronic payments systems – and issues relating to privacy of transactions – are viewed and addressed. This in turn depends on social norms and preferences that differ strongly across countries. In most countries, cash is likely to be a feature of retail payments systems for a sufficiently long time for

---

84  Denmark has such restrictions but has recently considered lifting them. Sweden does not have such restrictions, which may partly explain the quicker move to going cashless in Sweden.
85  See Segendorf and Wretman (2015) for examples of such policies in the case of Sweden.
86  Central bank reserve accounts are currently held only by banks, mainly for historical reasons.
87  For a discussion of such a role for the authorities in the case of Sweden, see Segendorf and Wretman (2015).

it to be worthwhile considering raising the inflation target, as proposed in the previous chapter. Adopting a periodical review process for the inflation target would allow central banks to adjust targets over time while minimising the associated risk of credibility loss.

# 6 Conclusions: So what should be done?

Large-scale asset purchases (quantitative easing) and negative nominal policy interest rates make recent central bank policies in advanced economies appear exceptional. Yet these measures are not unorthodox. Instead they are better thought of as the projection of an entirely conventional approach to monetary policy onto a post-recession environment of low inflation and slow recovery. After all, raising and lowering the cost of financing through operating in asset markets has been the *modus operandi* of central banks for centuries.

Determined to ease financing conditions to the extent necessary to meet their mandates, central banks have proved that zero does not represent a hard lower bound for nominal interest rates. They have shown that large-scale outright purchases of long-term or risky securities are effective in lowering term and risk premiums, thereby increasing asset prices and boosting aggregate demand.

These measures have had a macroeconomic effect: output and employment have recovered to a greater degree than they would have done without the policies. Nonetheless, the recoveries of output and employment have been slow compared to past deep recessions, and the recovery is still incomplete in many economies, most notably the Eurozone and Japan.

Although not unlimited, and not free of side-effects, these tools are far from being exhausted. The liquidity trap has so far only hampered monetary policy; it has not made it ineffective. The idea that monetary policy doesn't matter has proved in history to be a most dangerous fallacy (Romer and Romer, 2013).

A central bank finding itself with below target inflation and insufficient aggregate demand can:

1. Push nominal policy rates below zero. Rates can go substantially lower – perhaps temporarily even as low as –2%. Lower rates would generate a stronger stimulus, and any adverse side-effects would be manageable. The quicker the downturn can be reversed, the shorter the needed duration of negative interest rates.

2. Expand the scale and scope of asset purchases (QE). While the scope for using QE varies somewhat across economies, depending on financial market structure and legal restrictions on central bank powers, the likely adverse side-effects (for example, in terms of exposing the central bank to financial losses) are much less significant than is sometimes thought. Aggressive QE could deliver macroeconomic stimulus equivalent to a cut in the policy interest rate of anywhere from 2 to 6 percentage points, and possibly more.

3. Consider moving – even temporarily – to a higher inflation target. By itself, such an announcement might not be credible if the existing target is being undershot. However, if backed up by the actions listed under (1) and (2), it could increase expected inflation and thereby lower the effective real interest rate for a given nominal rate.

Some central banks may consider that they are getting back on target. Still, even for these, the downward secular trend in the neutral level of real interest rates (Bean et al., 2015), combined with the existing inflation targets at around 2%, is sure to increase the frequency with which the lower bound re-emerges in the future. As a result, economies are more likely to undershoot macroeconomic goals – less than full employment risks become chronic.

The continued appropriateness of the existing inflation target clearly deserves reconsideration in light of this prospect. A formalised review of the inflation target, assessing both costs and benefits of a change, should be undertaken in each country or currency area on a periodic basis to ensure that the tools of monetary policy have the necessary room for manoeuvre in downturns, taking into account national circumstances that may influence the optimal rate of inflation.

The growing use of electronic payments is making cash less and less necessary in the modern economy. A gradual transition to a world without cash is all but inevitable, and will be a less profound change than the shift from commodity money to fiat money. Although the abandonment of cash altogether is not an immediate prospect, technological trends, which can be encouraged by regulators, bring that eventuality closer while still enabling social inclusion in the payments system to be assured. In a cashless society there is no obvious lower bound to nominal interest rates and monetary policy can more easily act to halt and reverse an economic downturn.

Although this report addresses the tools of monetary policy, there is no denying that the task of the central bank in conditions of low demand and low or negative inflation is made harder by insufficient use of fiscal policy. The re-emergence of 'helicopter money' proposals – for example, involving the central bank in the transfer of spending power to households – represents one possible approach to generating stimulus in a liquidity trap. A better policy mix would surely generate a better overall economic performance.

# Discussions

## The Geneva Report: Overview

### Comments by the discussants

**Donald Kohn,** *The Brooking Institution*
Donald Kohn felt that this report couldn't be more timely or important. One of the narratives that has taken hold and contributed to roiling global markets in the early part of 2016 is that central banks were running out of room to use even unconventional policies to boost growth, dooming the global economy to a prolonged period of resource under-utilisation and inflation rates well below central bank targets.

This report is a very helpful and comprehensive guide to monetary policy in a liquidity trap – at the zero lower bound for policy rates. It aggregates and evaluates the many studies of the effects of unconventional polices undertaken in the past several years, marshals new evidence on the effects of negative policy rates, and uses those results to make concrete suggestions for policy at the zero lower bound, which it tests in a number of counterfactual exercises

The authors arrive at several conclusions:
1. The zero lower bound and liquidity trap are far more likely to be issues in the future than in the past, given the decline of the equilibrium short-term interest rate.
2. Just about everything central banks tried in terms of low/negative interest rates and asset purchases/QE worked to ease financial conditions, and by extension to bolster growth and prevent even worse outcomes, and the negative side effects, if any, have been small and far outweighed by the benefits of these policies.
3. So to escape the liquidity traps today and in the future, the advice to central banks is to just do more – lower more, buy more, buy over a wider array of assets.
4. And while they are at it, central banks should drive inflation rates to new higher targets of, say, 4% to elevate nominal rates and make episodes at the zero lower bound less frequent.

Kohn's comment was of the character "yes, but". He broadly agreed with many of the conclusions reached by the authors, but thought there are nuances, costs and complications they could examine more carefully and that central banks need to consider when making policy in a liquidity trap or raising their inflation targets.

*Kohn agreed that central banks are likely to find themselves dealing with liquidity traps more in the future than in the past.* Sluggish growth in potential GDP, reflecting slower technological change, weak capital investment and the demographics of aging populations, has contributed to a prolonged decline in r*. *But he cautioned*

*that future episodes in the liquidity trap may be less serious than one might infer from recent history, and this different character could have implications for policies at the zero lower bound.* That's because of the very substantial beefing up of the regulation of the financial sector in the wake of the global financial crisis. Standards for bank capital, liquidity and risk management have been raised quite substantially; plans for bank resolution that minimise risks to financial stability are being made; and some non-bank markets that contributed to financial instability in 2008 have been made more transparent and safer, for example through the use of central counterparties for clearing.

This regulation probably has contributed to the decline in r* by making intermediation more expensive. But it also means that the amplification of real economy shocks by the financial sector is considerably less likely, and when it occurs should be less serious. Well-capitalised and highly liquid banks will be much less subject to runs with forced fire sales of assets; interconnections in derivative markets will be more transparent and the risk easier to manage; and credit should keep flowing to the real economy following an adverse development. Of course, business and financial cycles will persist, fuelled by waves of greed and fear and miscalculations by private and public sectors, but the resulting recessions are more likely to be of the garden variety type, with implications for time spent in a liquidity trap and perhaps for the appropriate type of response.

*Kohn agreed that unconventional monetary policies have been effective at easing financial conditions and boosting the economy.* The report concentrates a lot on the policy of quantitative easing – 'large-scale asset purchases', in Fed jargon. The authors identify three channels through which such purchases should work. First, a market-calming channel in which central bank purchases help to restore market liquidity when trading conditions are disrupted. Second, purchases can reinforce the signals that the central bank is sending about its intention to keep interest rates at unusually low levels for unusually long periods. Third is the portfolio balance channel, in which central bank purchase of longer-term or risker assets reduces term or risk premiums directly and which is transmitted more widely as the previous holders of these assets rebalance their portfolios.

*But, Kohn wondered whether the report's conclusions about the effectiveness of QE derived from recent experience will be applicable to future episodes of liquidity traps and if they are not, what that says about the efficacy and ordering of unconventional policy tools.* Without a doubt, the Fed's first quantitative easing in a dysfunctional MBS market was highly effective. But, as he noted, financial disruption is likely to be much milder in future episodes, reducing any impact from the market-calming channel.

With regard to signalling future policy intentions, central banks have developed various means of forward guidance for policy interest rates over this episode of policy at the zero lower bound. Guidance has become more sophisticated and more economy-based, as, in Kohn's view, it should be. The Fed and other central banks have seen forward guidance as a key element and a separate tool from purchases in unconventional policy, and it will come into play in a more developed state in the next episode, reducing the need for and impact of the signalling channel for QE.

Trimming expected future short-term rates is a powerful tool for convincing households and businesses to bring future spending forward to the present, as it emphasises that yields on holding liquid assets into the future are going to present a poor alternative use of funds to spending today. The report barely touches on the experience of central banks with forward guidance and its efficacy in promoting spending; greater attention to this tool would enhance the utility of this report for researchers and central banks.

That portfolio balance channel will continue to have effects on term and risk premiums – depending on the type and duration of the assets purchased. The question is just how powerful this will be in stimulating spending if purchases have no effect on market functioning and little effect on expected short-term rates, given the use also of forward guidance. QE should remain effective to some extent; for example, it will increase incentives to borrow and it will raise asset prices, activating a wealth channel. But with expected rates little affected, the impact of the portfolio balance channel by itself on bringing spending forward could be muted. And that might affect the most effective ordering and mix of unconventional policies in a liquidity trap.

Asset purchases generally also involve the central bank taking some fiscal risk. This is true even when the assets purchased are longer-term government bonds without credit risk, as the Fed has been doing. The expected profits from holding long-term government obligations financed with short-term debt (bank reserves) will be positive because of the term premiums that were prevalent when the central bank undertook its purchases. But the returns on carry trades can vary considerably – that's why there are term premiums under normal circumstances. And of course, purchases of corporate bonds or private mortgage securities or equities entail much more risk as well as decisions about government intervention credit allocation that are normally made by the fiscal authorities.

*So Kohn's second "yes, but" for unconventional policies is to consider the governance and accountability issues of independent central banks engaging in QE.* Governments and central banks have found ways to deal with this during the crisis for some of the facilities. For example, the Fed's TALF facility which lent against private securitisations came with a backstop from the Treasury's TARP programme; and the Bank of England's corporate bond purchases were made pursuant to a public letter form the Chancellor concerning compensation for any loses. Discomfort at the Federal Reserve with some of these issues was reflected in an 'accord' with the Treasury department in the spring of 2009, acknowledging (among other things) the temporary allocative implications of intervening in government-backed MBS markets. Questions have also been raised about the debt management implications of the Federal Reserve's purchase of long-term Treasury securities – how should this be coordinated in the future with the debt managers at the Treasury department?

In sum, QE raises serious issues of governance and accountability for independent central banks that should at least be acknowledged and discussed if public and legislative support for central bank independence in the conduct of monetary policy is to be maintained. Kohn suspected that one reason some central banks were slower to adopt QE types of policies was their concern about provoking questions regarding authority and independence; better these issues be confronted openly in dialogue with legislators.

*He agreed that a 4% inflation target that was achieved and credibly committed to would have substantial benefits because it would materially lower the odds on future liquidity traps and encounters with the zero lower bound, given the higher average level of nominal interest rates implied by a higher target.* Of course, there are costs to weigh against these benefits. The report argues convincingly that some of the often cited costs can be reduced over time. One such cost is the greater variability of higher levels of inflation. Another is the concern that raising the inflation target will undermine the credibility of any such target – raising it once will arouse suspicions that it can be changed and make it much harder to build credibility for the new target. Both of these can be overcome by central bank actions, though it may take some time and entail transition costs advocates of higher targets rarely consider. For example, building credibility for a 4% target is likely to require leaning extra hard against any tendencies for inflation to overshoot this objective for a while. This kind of asymmetrical reaction function implies that embedding 4% is likely to require inflation averaging below 4% for some time.

*But more broadly, higher inflation could well have costs that go beyond these last two or the 'shoe leather', menu, and tax distortion costs the report discusses.* Alan Greenspan defined price stability as "best thought of as an environment in which inflation is so low and stable over time that it does not materially enter into the decisions of households and firms". That definition has resonated with many over the years. It reflects, in Kohn's view, recognition that inflation has costs beyond the technical issues already discussed. It complicates decision-making and distorts market signals. Also, higher inflation probably creates difficulties for households and businesses with limited financial expertise in particular, and is likely to have disproportionate effects on small businesses who can't hire that expertise and on less-educated households.

This sense of broader costs could be one reason 'price stability' is so deeply entrenched in legislation and treaties that establish central bank mandates; 4% is not price stability in that the price level would double every 18 years. The benefits could well exceed the costs in a world of r* close to zero. But at a minimum, good governance and accountability would suggest consultation with the legislature or other authorising authority so the costs and benefits could be fully aired by elected officials.

*Finally, Kohn agreed that unconventional policies at the zero lower bound have been effective, but what lessons should we draw from the experience of Japan?* Japan seems to be a distinct natural experiment in the all-in use of unconventional policies to escape a liquidity trap. Under its current governor, the Bank of Japan has used all the tools advocated by the authors of the report and used them aggressively, but it has not had the kind of success one might have anticipated from reading the report. It raised its inflation target (to 2% percent from 1%); it has purchased large quantities of both government and private longer-term obligations, including equities in the form of ETFs; and it has reduced its target rate into negative territory. Many financial market measures responded, at least initially. Core inflation rose for a while, albeit partly reflecting the rise in the level of import prices after the yen depreciated, and inflation expectations also increased. But progress stopped well short of the 2% target and recent signs are that the higher inflation has not become entrenched in wages and that core is slipping back – though it remains higher than before the programme began. Perhaps the Bank of Japan should just do more of everything, as the report implies, but it is

troubling that more sustainable success at hitting a higher target has not been achieved; the Japanese experience is worthy of extra study for its implications for what works to overcome a liquidity trap.

**Frank Smets,** *European Central Bank*
Frank Smets broadly agreed with the authors' conclusions. The report convincingly shows that the effective lower bound is a constraint that has produced some costs. Yet, there are a number of unconventional tools that can partially substitute and complement the short-term interest rate. These include negative rates, asset purchase programmes and targeted lending. It is worth further exploring targeted lending in the report. In a bank-based economy, like the Eurozone, targeted lending has been a powerful tool to support transmission through the bank-lending channel. While the report acknowledges most negative side effects of unconventional tools, it lacks a discussion on whether they have an impact on the incentive for governments to pursue structural reforms or consolidate the government budget. Given the current debate in some Eurozone countries, this could be a useful addition to the report.

The authors argue that the benefits of unconventional policies exceed their costs and imply that central banks can move further in employing these tools. But, it is also worth acknowledging that some of the costs are likely to rise as the use of unconventional tools increases. For example, pushing negative rates into the territory suggested by the authors could result in counterproductive effects on the bank lending channel, especially in the Eurozone. It is therefore important to stress the role of other policies that can mitigate some of these costs.

The report seems to suggest a temporary increase in the inflation target. This might not be necessary and is difficult to communicate. Rather, targeting an average inflation rate would lead to similar results and be much easier to communicate. On the abolition of cash, one can doubt that cash will disappear. If cash were abolished, substitutes would likely appear.

The ECB's latest easing cycle started when downward risks to price stability materialised. The overall strategy has followed a three-pronged approach, consisting of reductions in the main policy rates and two non-standard measures, namely, targeted longer-term refinancing operations (TLTROs) and broad-based asset purchase programmes. Evidence shows that this strategy has been effective. The yield curve on government bonds has flattened and fallen dramatically between June 2014 and May 2016. The easing cycle has also had an effect on other financial markets, whereby a large part of the easing can be attributed to monetary policy, and can account for about half of the growth in the Eurozone economy in 2015 and 2016. These effects are in the same ballpark as those in the United States and the United Kingdom. As to the impact of low interest rates on bank profitability, it is worth highlighting that the negative effects on interest rate margins have, on average, been compensated by capital gains, improvements in credit quality in the form of lower loan losses, and a rise in the quantity of credit

# Three questions

## 1. Can non-standard policies do it?

**Kiyohiko Nishimura,** *University of Tokyo and Graduate Institute for Policy Studies*
As former Deputy Governor of the Bank of Japan during the global financial crisis of 2008, Kiyohiko Nishimura cannot help feeling that the draft report seems to be trying to re-institute the pre-global financial crisis consensus. In particular, (a) it assumes stable and significant effects of real interest rates on aggregate demand, though the effects may be somewhat lowered); (b) financial stability issues are assumed to be not so important, when the economy is trapped in stagnation; and (c) it assumes that central banks' credibility is still maintained to influence inflationary expectations.

The basic message of the draft report is, first, that with the help of negative interest rates recently added, QE improves monetary policy effectiveness even under the zero bound constraint, through significantly lowering long rates for lending and borrowing, and through resulting wealth effects on stock and property markets. Second, however, the zero bound still poses serious problems, since it make it difficult to lower real interest rates as deeply and swiftly as desired in the case of large negative shocks like the ones we have had. This implies that we have to do more of both in quantity and quality at the same time.

Nishimura first examined the authors' assessment of negative interest rates as policy. The authors are generally very positive about this new addition of unconventional policies. He agreed with them that negative policy rates *per se* are a natural extension of the traditional interest rate policy, as they circumvent some (though not all) of the constraints of zero lower bounds. Their analysis suggests that a swift lowering of these rates is effective in restoring equilibrium and in returning to normal positive rates. However, they do not examine how the negative interest policy is communicated to the public and the financial markets, and how the communication affects the effectiveness of the policy itself. Nishimura believes the communication issue is very important in assessing the negative rate policy. As a policy, the negative rate policy should not only be crafted carefully but also communicated to the public well in advance.

Unfortunately, it is not always the case, and this hampers the effectiveness of this new policy tool. Negative policy rates necessitate adjustment in financial institutions whose systems are not built to incorporate negative interest rates, and business practices such as swaps should be changed accordingly. It takes time, and some say maybe more than six months. Thus, the policy change of negative interest rates should not have been introduced as a surprise move as the Bank of Japan did.

Moreover, the surprise move also posed a serious communication problem for the central bank. Consumers' reaction to negative interest rates is overwhelmingly negative, though somewhat irrationally, since consumers seem to take negative interest rates as a visible and unjust punishment on savers to prepare for future uncertainty. Consumers' apathy possibly hampers the credibility of the central bank, at a time when this credibility is absolutely necessary for the central bank to raise people's inflationary expectations. This is all the more serious since consumers' attitudes and expectations show a considerable 'hysteresis' or very slow adaptation. Thus, it compromises the ability of the central bank to act timely.

Problems of financial markets and institutions will be resolved as time passes, but people's negative reaction lingers to prevent the central bank from, for example, going deeper into negative territory to jump-start the economy. Other central banks face similar communication policy challenges when they go into the negative range.

Nishimura then turned to the authors' presumption of stable and still significant effects of real interest rates on aggregate demand, Assumption (a). To examine the validity of this assumption, he took up Japan as an example, which he knows better than other economies. The effects of real interest rate changes on aggregate demand are apparently trending down, especially sharply after the massive quantitative and qualitative easing (QQE) started in April 2013. It is called QQE since the Bank of Japan not only buys sovereign debts massively, but also purchases stocks and properties indirectly through ETF and REIT.

Figure 1 is taken from the Bank of Japan's most recent *Outlook for Economic Activity and Prices* (April 2016). It juxtaposes investment (I/K) (thick line) and the real interest gap (thin line), which is the difference between the actual and so-called natural interest rate in a reverse scale between 1995 to date. 1995 is the year in which the problem of non-performing loans gradually surfaced, but full-blown financial crisis was still a couple of years away. The figure suggests that the effect of the real interest rate on investment has decreased significantly after the QQE. A large decline in the actual real interest rate, that is, a large real interest rate gap, has generated a comparable increase in investment until April 2013. Since the announcement of QQE, in contrast, a large real interest rate gap produces only a mediocre increase in investment. The same story applies to consumption expenditure. As shown in Figure 2, although the significant decrease in the real interest rate spurs a sizable increase in property prices as expected, it fails to ignite consumption expenditure. At the time of writing, consumption shows a sign of decline.

**Figure 1**   Real interest rate change and investment in Japan: Sharply declined effectiveness after QQE (dashed vertical line)

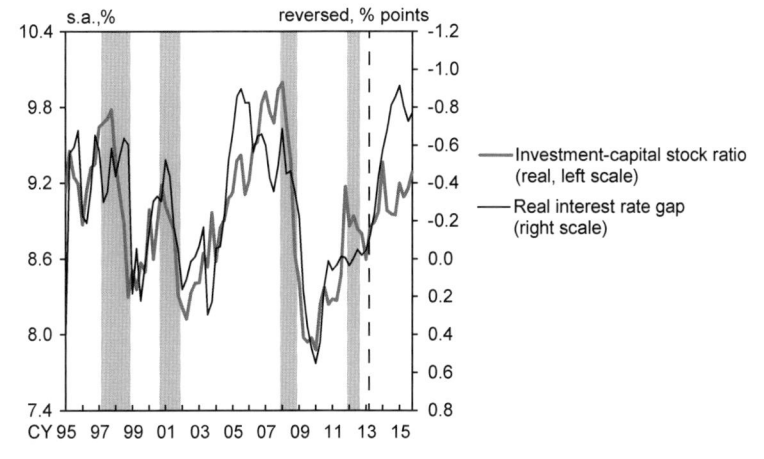

*Notes:* Real interest rate gap = real interest rate - natural interest rate (both are based on 10-year JGB yields). For details, see "The Natural Yield Curve: Its Concept and Measurement," Bank of Japan Working Paper Series, 15-E-5.

*Source:* Bank of Japan (2016).

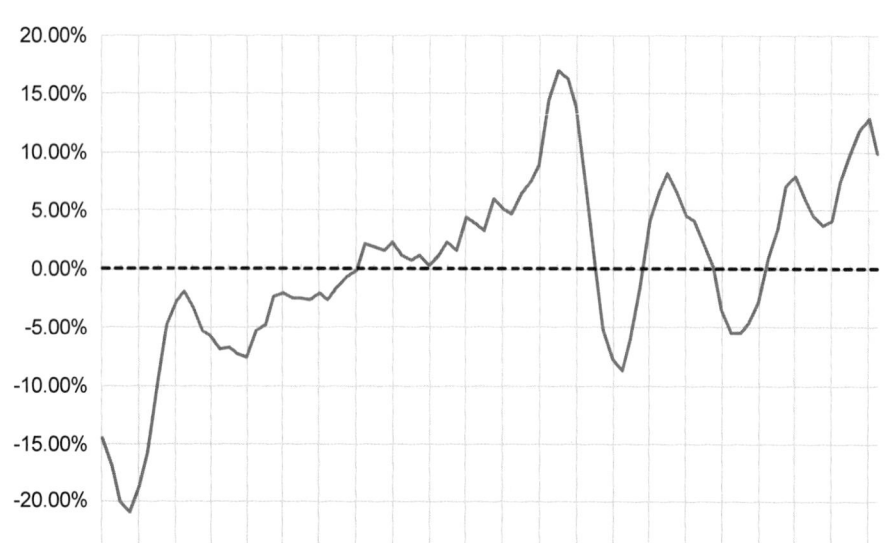

**Figure 2**  Property price inflation (year on year) in Japan: Real interest rate is still effective here, however...

Consequently, in spite of the massive QQE (and fiscal stimulus of so-called Abenomics), Japanese GDP growth has been trending down significantly after the QQE of April 2013, as seen in Figure 3, which presents year-on-year real GDP growth from 1995 to date. Real GDP growth has been trending down after QQE. After the global financial crisis and its aftermath (2008-2011) and before QQE (2013), the average growth rate in the period of 2011 and 2012 is 0.68%. This is the period of the devastation of the northern Japan earthquake and ensuing very slow recovery due to the effect of Fukushima, so that it is hardly a period of favourable conditions for growth. However, the average year-on-year growth of 0.56% after QQE is even lower than during the earthquake period. Ironically, growth becomes weaker as QQE expands further.

Japan may be a little bit extreme, but the sensitivity of aggregate demand components to monetary policy tools seems to be decreasing in many other economies as well. The change is likely brought by an interaction of common global factors such as ageing populations, employment-unfriendly information and communication technology, and severe balance-sheet adjustment after a property bubble.[74]

---

[74] Nishimura refers to these factors as three seismic changes in the global economy, and explains their effects in Nishimura (2016).

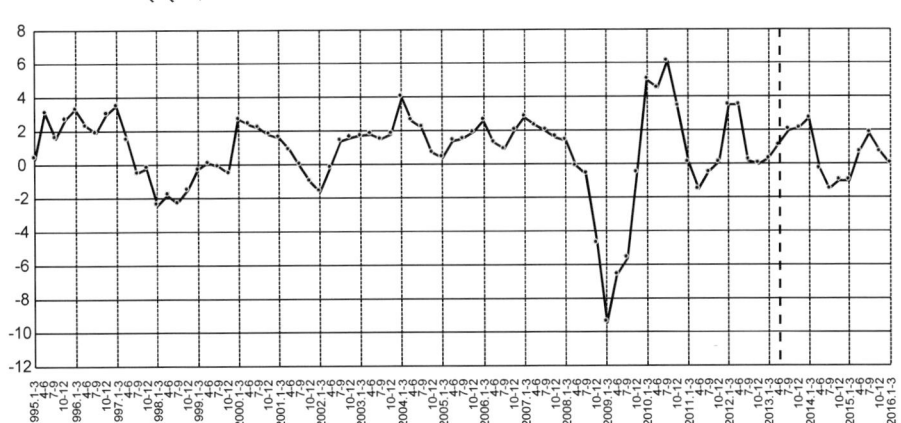

**Figure 3**  Real GDP growth (year on year) in Japan: Significant trending down after QQE (vertical dashed line)

It seems that marginal returns on QE policy have rapidly decreased because external conditions became unfavourable. Thus unfortunately, it seems that QE might be overwhelmed by policy exhaustion, and this makes things worse. Financial markets are increasingly aware of the possibility of policy exhaustion. When market participants see possible signs of policy exhaustion, the intended effect of a particular QE move is easily erased, and even reversed, by the expectations that no further effective QE action is possible in the future.

Market reactions to negative interest rates in Japan on 29 January 2016 are a manifestation of this effect. Their initial reaction was a yen depreciation, as expected by the Bank of Japan. However, that effect dissipated quickly and markets moved decisively in the opposite direction. Market commentaries at that time suggested that the introduction of negative rates was a sign of policy exhaustion and an inability to deliver effective QE measures. In order to counter policy exhaustion, central banks are obliged to pledge more actions just to preserve the initially intended effect.

It is increasingly clear that many economies are rapidly approaching policy exhaustion. It may not be an immediate concern in the US, which underlies the authors' argument. However, Nishimura senses that even the US is getting closer to this point. What kind of policy prescription do the authors have in mind in the presence of policy exhaustion?

Finally, Nishimura considered another issue, not fully analysed in the report – financial stability, or assumption (b). Here again, the issue is most vividly present in Japan. QQE has transformed profoundly long maturity JGB markets, which historically provided a yardstick of risk-free long rates. At the time of writing, market participants often point out that the only game in town – Japanese government bond (JGB) markets – is the so-called Bank of Japan trade. Since the Bank of Japan purchases more JGBs than are newly issued, many banks (especially mega-banks) have already sold their sizable stocks. Typical trades found in the JGB markets right now consist of buying JGBs from the government to sell then to the Bank of Japan, often immediately. The market participants' only concern is the rate at which the Bank of Japan purchases their JGBs.

82  What Else Can Central Banks Do?

Before QQE, long-maturity JGB markets were where market participants guessed other market participants' assessment of long-term risk free rates. (At that time, the Bank of Japan purchased JGBs, but only for short-term ones.) The market rates represented market participants' 'collective' expectations of the risk-free rates in the future. Since market participants could and did arbitrage between different maturities, the expectation theory based on arbitrage considerations provided a convenient framework to understand the yield curve of risk-free rates. This is the price-discovery function of sovereign bond markets. The massive QQE has reduced this price discovery function considerably.

The extreme flattening of JGB yield curves after negative rates are introduced on January 29, depicted in Figure 4, illustrates the loss of the price-discovery function. It shows the transition of JGB yield curves over time. The flattening started gradually after the September MPM of 2015 (a change from the black dotted line of September to the black thin line of January 28). This could still be explained in a traditional expectation theoretic framework, in that market participants began to realise that zero policy rates would remain longer than previously expected because inflation failed to show upward momentum. However, the change after the negative rate announcement of January 29 is so extreme that it is hard to explain with the expectation theory framework. The rates declined by almost as much as the rate on commercial banks' so-called policy rate balances at the Bank of Japan, and the decline was almost the same from one year to seven years. Moreover, the longer the maturity, the larger the decrease (20 years and 30 years).

**Figure 4**   Extreme flattening of JGB yield curve 'Bank of Japan trade' and lost price-discovery function

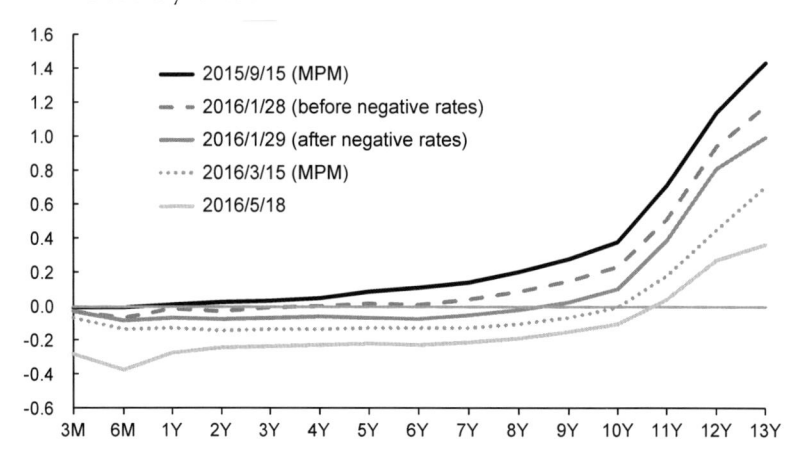

The only explanation Nishimura can give is that the negative interest rate policy destroyed the 'focal point' of market participants' expectations (which were still based on expectation theory) and that market participants were trying to rebuild the focal point by guessing the Bank of Japan's purchase rate. The 20-basis point change in the rate on policy rate balances led market participants to guess that the purchase rate change was also reduced by 20 basis points for shorter maturity bonds and that long rates were likely to be lowered by the same amount. This is the impact of 'Bank of Japan trade'.

Since risk-free rates in sovereign bond markets are reference rates on actual lending, a sharp decline in these sovereign rates induce a sharp decline in lending rates. In fact, the average new lending rate of all banks has been reduced by 20 basis points as well, from 0.920% in December to 0.705% in March. Since interest rates on deposits face a legal zero bound, banks' profitability will be reduced. The longer the negative interest rate policy remains, the more harmful it becomes for financial stability. In this respect, persistent negative interest rates will eventually pose a serious financial stability problem.

The conclusion is that the current combination of negative interest rates and large-scale purchases of long-maturity sovereign bonds creates a serious financial stability issue. Although Japan is an extreme example, Nishimura believes a similar problem is, or will eventually be, present in other countries where large-scale asset purchases make the central bank a whale in a pond. The problem is real, not simply a theoretical possibility.

## 2. Should the inflation target be raised?

**Ugo Panizza,** *The Graduate Institute*
Should the inflation target be raised? This is really two questions. The first question has to do with the optimal level of inflation, and the second relates to the credibility costs linked to tinkering with the inflation target.

What is the optimal level of inflation? This is a difficult question that was already being discussed by Milton Friedman, James Tobin and Edmund Phelps when Ugo Panizza had barely graduated from kindergarten. While Friedman's (1969) analysis found that the optimal rate of inflation is negative, successive work by Phelps (1973) suggested an optimal rate of inflation at around zero. Tobin's (1972) Presidential Address at the American Economic Association did not point to any specific value for the optimal rate of inflation, but described the benefits of moderate positive inflation by stating that: "No one has devised a way of controlling average wage rates without intervening in the competitive struggle over relative wages. Inflation lets this struggle proceed, and blindly, impartially, impersonally, and non-politically scales down all its outcomes." A positive inflation target is also consistent with more recent work by Akerlof et al. (1996), Wyplosz (2001) and Benigno and Ricci (2011). These authors find that that the long-run Phillips curve becomes positively sloped at low levels of inflation.

So, the inflation target should be positive. But, what should its level be? Ball (2013) conducts a careful cost-benefit analysis of raising the inflation target to 4% and finds that the benefits of such a policy (mostly linked to the decreased likelihood of hitting the zero lower bound) greatly outweigh its costs. Panizza tends to agree with this analysis and with the fact that an inflation target in the 3-4% range is preferable to a 2% target.

This takes us to the second question. Even if 4% is preferable to 2%, aren't there credibility costs linked to tinkering with the target? If we could identify a representative central banker, credibility costs would probably be the main argument against changing the target (e.g. Bernanke, 2010). Panizza is not persuaded by the importance of these credibility costs. They could be addressed by increasing the target and appointing a conservative central banker (Rogoff, 1985) who will fight hard against overshooting and raising the target (as central bankers are fighting against raising the target right now).

Other often-heard arguments against raising the target now are: (i) we need more thinking about this issue, and such an important decision should not be made at times of crisis; and (ii) what is the point of raising the target to 4% if we are not even able to get to 2%? Panizza is not persuaded by these two arguments either.

The first argument is standard for those who want to protect the status quo. During crisis periods, they suggest they say that crises are not a good time to change things, and when the crisis is over, they resort to "if ain't broke, don't fix it." The second argument is in contrast with the theoretical work of Krugman (1998) and Eggerston and Woodford (2003), who have shown that a way to achieve the 2% target is to commit *ex ante* to stay above the target longer than what would be optimal *ex post*. However, a higher target should allow going above the old 2% target and escape the liquidity trap.

Krugman (1998) and Eggerston and Woodford (2003) also bring us back to the credibility problem. Right now, central banks in advanced economies do not lack the credibility to keep inflation low enough. To the contrary, they lack the credibility to achieve higher inflation. If the solution to high inflation brought about by limited credibility was a conservative central banker, maybe the solution to the opposite problem is a 'hippy' central banker (i.e. a central banker who dislikes inflation less than society at large). In Paul Krugman's words, such a hippy central banker could "commit to being irresponsible" and bring us back to the 2% target.

If we need to choose between a 4% target with a conservative central banker and a 2% target with a hippy central banker, most economists would agree that 4% is better.

## 3. Is there a lower bound in a cashless economy?

**John Hassler,** *Stockholm University*

Is there a lower bound in a cashless society? From a textbook perspective, the answer is relatively straightforward. The nominal interest rate is the cost of holding money. At zero cost, demand is arbitrarily large, putting an effective zero lower bound. Without cash, this mechanism disappears. However, it is not entirely clear how monetary policy would work in a cashless society. The power of the central bank relies on its ability to create means of payment.

A related question is whether there is a zero lower bound in a 'cash-lean' society. Sweden, for example, is on its way to becoming a cashless society. In 1950, cash in circulation in Sweden was 10% of GDP. Since then, it has fallen to around 1.5% of GDP. In recent years, the fall has accelerated despite the low and now negative central bank policy rates.

Manifestations of this trend are that the average size of credit card transactions has fallen rapidly and that the Swedish real-time mobile payment service, SWISH, has expanded quickly since its introduction in 2012. It is becoming increasingly common for establishments to not accept cash. These developments are likely to continue.

There are several market forces driving this trend. Cash is costly and often considered inconvenient relative to electronic money. Moreover, cash is risky. Even banks prefer not to use cash and a large share of bank offices do not have cash at all. The Swedish are friendly to new technologies and shows a high level of trust; they are not worried about leaving trails from spending electronic money.

Policy is another force behind the trend towards a cashless society. Regulations against money laundering make transactions above US$1,000 complicated. In addition, the Swedish Riksbank distributes cash from a single distribution centre, with banks having to pay for the transport themselves.

An important question is whether the limited use of cash implies that the lower bound on interest rates has ceased to bind. The answer is likely negative.

So far, it has been possible to reduce rates to negative territory without money being hoarded. Both infrastructure and traditions have changed in a way that makes it unlikely to see a sudden increase in the use of cash. This provides some room to further decrease the policy rate, especially since the transmission mechanism appears to work as usual. Yet, deposit rates for households are not negative. Negative interbank rates therefore create a profit squeeze on banks. There are two possible explanations for why deposit rates have not turned negative. One is that some sort of money illusion might prevent banks from going into negative territory. Another reason might be that banks are worried that customers would start taking out cash if deposit rates were negative. Given that dealing with cash is costly and complicated, many banks might rather have a zero rate. Another concern for monetary policy is that Swedish banks dispose of reserves amounting to four times the cash in circulation. If rates were sufficiently low, banks could demand their reserves in cash.

The smooth trend towards a cashless society has been beneficial for Sweden. Suddenly removing cash to eliminate the zero lower bound would be dangerous, however. Money – both electronic and paper – requires trust. This trust is easy to break and hard to establish. If policy rates are expected to be negative for a long time, it cannot be ruled out that banks will reinvest in infrastructure for using more cash again demanding the reserves back as cash. The conclusion is: cash-lean is quite different from cashless.

## General discussion

Responding to comments on raising the inflation target, **Laurence Ball** noted that the costs of changing the target are likely to be low relative to the benefits. While the idea of losing Alan Greenspan's concept of price stability has a lot of intuitive appeal, we do not know how large the cost associated with it would be. Drawing on the example of retirement planning, he acknowledged that an inflation level of 4% instead of 2%, implying that the price level would double every 18 years, would add some complication. However, unemployment complicates retirement planning to a much larger degree. Hence, if raising the inflation target means fewer liquidity traps and less economic stagnation, the benefits would greatly outweigh the costs. Concerning the transition costs mentioned by Ugo Panizza, he argued that the transition to lower inflation in the early 1980s undertaken by Paul Volcker involved some costs. Nonetheless, today we would agree that this was the right decision. The costs of going from 2% to 4% are unlikely to be greater than they were then and would be small compared to the benefits of reduced economic stagnation.

**Joseph Gagnon** responded to Kiyohiko Nishimura that until nine months ago, Japan has been an incredibly supportive example of what is stated in the report. Following a new programme, core inflation rose by 200 basis points after stagnating below zero for a long time. Nothing besides the action of the Bank of Japan can explain this. During the past nine months, in contrast, no further

progress has been made. The move to negative rates was small and did not persuade markets. Our deeply rooted belief that expanding money supply causes inflation is based on a long history. We should not all of a sudden question this. What might be going on instead is that secular stagnation is pushing down the real interest rate. Not responding quickly enough leads to a deflationary trap. For policy to work, central banks have to buy assets with a positive rate of return, which are not perfect substitutes for money. With ten-year bond yields at zero, Japan is getting into a liquidity trap even on the long end, implying that it needs to turn to other assets.

Part of the subsequent discussion focused on the limits to monetary policy. **Avinash Persaud** expressed concerns about asking too much from central banks and their unconventional policies. These policies have been effective at lowering long-term interest rates, but they do not seem to have boosted business investment. The cost of funding is important for investment, but another vital factor is investment opportunity. Unconventional policies have boosted asset prices, which might be a factor lowering investment opportunity and thus investment spending. **Alexander Swoboda** agreed that it is extremely important not to overburden monetary policy with tasks it cannot achieve. The report should insist more on other policies, such as fiscal and structural policies. We expect too much from central banks and, maybe, they have promised too much.

**Claudio Borio** pointed out that raising the target might not necessarily reduce the likelihood of hitting the lower bound. It could be that, paradoxically, the reason why we are at the lower bound is that the inflation target is too high. Our models may well overestimate the ability of central banks to meet their inflation target, regardless of zero lower bound issues. In contrast to what Joseph Gagnon said, the Japanese experience is a possible reminder of that. If, for instance, monetary policy had just a temporary effect on the price level but not on the inflation rate, pushing policies to hit the inflation target might lead to a situation in which interest rates fall further and inflation goes back to its original level. In this situation, it is easy to hit the lower bound. We therefore need to have a broader analysis on the drivers of inflation. Factors such as technological change and globalisation are underestimated. The experience of Japan is not supportive of the idea that low inflation destroys the economy; its unemployment rate is very low and growth is above potential. This raises the question of whether we should continue pursuing unconventional policies just because of inflation. When and where should we stop and what is the limit to what monetary policy can do? Alternatively, why should governments not finance themselves with very short-term bills? In a related comment, **Alexander Swoboda** remarked that choosing the inflation target is not independent from achieving it. If we want the inflation target to be consistent with achieving the central bank's mandate, we should probably choose a low target. Likewise, **Luigi Buttiglione** wondered why we are discussing increasing the inflation target, given that central banks cannot currently meet it. Moreover, he would have liked to see a discussion of the transmission of negative rates through the exchange rate channel in the report. **Thomas Moser** added that the liquidity trap is related to the real long-term interest rate. The effective lower bound is a sufficient condition for a liquidity trap, but not a necessary condition. Hence, a cashless society eliminates the lower bound but not necessarily the liquidity trap.

**Laurence Ball** acknowledged that the report should have addressed the idea that there might be a lack of good investment opportunities. However, one has to differentiate between the slope of the IS curve and a shift in the IS curve. If there is a lack of investment opportunities, the IS curve shifts back, but this does not imply that there is no interest-sensitive spending in the economy. **Signe Krogstrup** noted that there has been a lot of misunderstanding related to the effectiveness of negative rates. These often aimed at responding to a reduction in inflation expectations. The negative rates did not outweigh the initial shocks that they were responding to. This has not been understood by the public and therefore has led to the wrong conclusion that negative rates are ineffective.

## Lessons from the financial markets

### Comments by the discussants

**Jean Boivin,** BlackRock
There is no doubt that monetary policy has been extremely effective at easing financial conditions. Monetary policy has clearly been reflected in the behaviour of asset managers. Over the last few months, however, market dynamics indicates that markets have concluded that monetary policy has reached a limit. For example, the increased correlation between oil prices and inflation expectations can be understood as a manifestation of markets having priced in the binding zero lower bound. Monetary policy works primarily through the expectation channel, and this channel is being questioned. If this is the case, monetary policy can be helpful for fine-tuning but not to address broader concerns related to the liquidity trap. Dealing with the liquidity trap requires a contingency plan that is not limited to monetary policy. In this sense, the report is too optimistic about the potential of monetary policy.

There might also exist a stigma around negative rates. A large share of bonds – 27% of the global bond universe – is in negative yields. In Switzerland, it extends to maturities of more than 17 years. While the report does a fantastic job in explaining how and why negative rates should work, it lacks the distinction between small and large open economies. For small open economies, negative rates are a more powerful tool because of the impact they have on the exchange rate. For large economies, in contrast, negative rates cannot have the same effect through the exchange rate. As far as responding to significant shocks, negative interest rates are pretty much exhausted. It is not clear why negative rates should be favoured over QE. In addition, there is no strong conviction from the central bank community to defend negative rates in the way it has defended asset purchases. This also contributes to doubts associated with the use of negative rates.

The report argues that there is no reason to expect a decreasing impact of monetary policy through the portfolio rebalancing channel. Easing monetary policy usually has an impact on demand when it is temporary. The substitution effect of lower interest rates then stimulates consumption. In the current environment, loose monetary policy is no longer of a temporary nature. The flatter the yield curve turns, the weaker the substitution effect. This might imply that the income effect is dominating the substitution effect. We might thus be in a situation in which the financial impact is significant, while the effect on the real economy is not that large. If growth does not materialise, some of these financial positions might create financial stability risks.

**Thomas Mayer,** Flossbach von Storch Research Institute
The authors of this interesting report employ a standard new Keynesian model to assess the effects of recent non-standard monetary policy measures on growth and inflation. They conclude that these measures worked, but should have been applied more forcefully. Thomas Mayer's concern about this approach is that the model may be wrong, and therefore the policy recommendation false.

Since the collapse of Lehman Brothers, we have learned that credit matters. Mayer's own research (in collaboration with Michael Biggs) shows that credit flows are closely correlated with demand flows, over long periods of time and in almost every country. Occasionally, credit even drives demand. Credit cycles are the result. In the last hundred years, the most pronounced credit cycles occurred from the late 1920s to the early 1930s, and the late 1990s to the end of the 2010s. Credit plays no role in the new Keynesian model, but it is a key driver of the business cycle in the Wicksell-Mises-Hayek (WMH) model. Had we paid closer attention to the WMH model, we probably would not have been caught unaware by the burst of the recent credit bubble. And were we to be paying attention to it now, we could learn that the present course of monetary policy most likely will not revive the economy, but rather will cement the distortions created during the upswing of the credit cycle and lay the ground for more trouble in the future.

The WMH model predicts further, and possibly even deeper financial crises, if the present course of policy is maintained. However, there are no signs of a change of theory in academics or of policy practice in central banks. For an asset management company such as the one Mayer works for, there is no other choice but to build a portfolio of robust assets that have a good chance to survive another financial crisis.

**Sushil Wadhwani,** *Wadhwani Asset Management LLP*
Within the report, there is next to no discussion of what the effects might be of changing the inflation target on equity markets. And yet these effects are critically important in evaluating whether the target should be changed. For example, one branch of the academic literature that examined the effect of inflation on equities – which originated in the 1970s – suggests that higher inflation hurts stock prices; indeed, during the 1960s, 1970s and 1980s, there was a close (positive) association between nominal yields and earnings yields. More recently, however, we may have entered a regime in which higher inflation *boosts* stock prices. In fact, textbook theory suggests that nominal rates of return on all assets should rise one-for-one with inflation. Besides, econometric evidence from the UK shows that a switch of sign in the relationship between inflation and equities appears to have happened in the early 2000s (e.g. Wadhwani, 2013). In a low (below-target) inflation environment, higher inflation seems to be favourable for equity prices. A better understanding of the impact of inflation on financial markets is required in evaluating such a major regime change.

Concerning QE, Wadhwani noted that financial market evidence suggests that the effects are beginning to diminish. This may be a signal that QE is becoming less effective. However, the evidence has been heterogeneous, particularly when looking at the impact on stock prices. While some differences, such as the difference between QE1 and QE2, are easily explicable, others are more puzzling. For example, it is not clear why there is a lack of a robust impact of QE on stock markets in the case of the United Kingdom. Likewise, empirical evidence on the effectiveness of QE in Japan is mixed. The impact of QE on inflation is underwhelming. Moreover, the Federal Reserve has continuously revised down its growth forecasts over the last six years. While both supply-side and demand-side disappointments play a role, it seems plausible that the efficacy of QE is also lower than expected.

On negative rates, Wadhwani encouraged the authors to look at Goodhart's new – or second – law. Negative rates reduce the income of banks. Since banks cannot pass on negative rates to retail customers, their interest margins get squeezed. This reduced profitability of banks constrains credit expansion. Hence, the only way for negative rates to be economically effective is to break the taboo around negative deposit rates. Unfortunately, that is politically impossible.

Finally, if the report is overly optimistic on QE, on negative rates and on the possibility of raising the inflation target, then there is clearly a need to consider other policy options. It seems that helicopter money is the only game in town. There are serious issues related to helicopter money, such as potential market instabilities and scare stories about hyperinflation and central banks losing independence. These are exactly those issues that need to be discussed alongside the big advantage of helicopter money – i.e. a greater stimulatory impact than conventional QE since lower bond yields, of themselves, have an uncertain stimulatory effect.

## General discussion

In response to Shushil Wadhwani, **Laurence Ball** stressed that it is important to make a distinction between inflation and the inflation target. The correlation between inflation and equity prices might be different, depending on whether the target is met or not. This is relevant to answer the question of whether the inflation target should be increased. Setting a higher target constitutes a challenge for communication. However, if it is communicated clearly, real interest rates are much lower once agents believe the new target can be reached. **Joseph Gagnon** added that QE has had an effect in Japan. Core inflation excluding energy prices has risen 200 basis points. It did not get Japan all the way to the Bank of Japan target, but two-thirds of the way to it. The markets now see that Japan is not willing to do more, and this is the reason why the effects unravel. Concerning Thomas Mayer's comment, he noted that low interest rates help restructuring. They push up asset prices and increase the asset side of the balance sheet.

**Gene Frieda** wondered about communication challenges. He asked whether communication has become more difficult and how we should use it going forward. **Carlo Monticelli** noted that not enough attention has been paid to the political economy of QE and negative rates. These entail redistributive effects and consequently require an explanation. It is not obvious how independent central banks, which base their independence on the notion that their policies have no redistributive effects, can communicate this.

**Eric Santor** was intrigued by Jean Boivin's comment about the need to treat the targets symmetrically. In a world were forecasts are repeatedly revised downwards, policymakers think it is better to approach the target from below. Would there be any use in deliberately overshooting the target to approach it symmetrically from above? In this way, there would be no need to change the target. **Jan Toth** agreed that rather than changing the inflation target, it might be helpful to approach it symmetrically. In addition, the target could be measured on the basis of a five-year average. **Gaston Gelos** was not persuaded by the claims that QE was not effective. The solution may have been to be a bit more forceful with QE during the recession. From a welfare perspective, a lower target may be quite desirable. The report could benefit from a fuller discussion of price level targeting.

**Jan Toth** was more optimistic on negative rates. We have learnt that it should be the first tool used when hitting the zero lower bound. Policymakers should overshoot at the beginning to limit the time spent in negative territory and thereby reduce financial stability concerns. **Luigi Buttiglione** mentioned that in the Eurozone it is not clear whether the effectiveness of QE has declined or whether there has been an issue of communication. **Edwin Truman** asked whether the discussants would rather run the experiment in reverse. Do they think we would be better off if we gave up QE and returned to positive rates? **Anthony Smouha** wondered whether there could be a discussion on the incentives for monetary policy transmission going forward.

**Eric Santor** noted that the report would be useful for central bankers if it had an informed discussion on helicopter money. In practice, it would require the central bank to give up control over its balance sheet on a permanent basis, and therefore potentially control over the ability to hit the inflation target. It could also result in fiscal dominance, which would undo central bank independence. Thus, it might be better to have a conversation about the right fiscal and monetary policy mix before thinking about helicopter money. **Alexander Swoboda** agreed with this remark. Helicopter money raises the question of whether it is about monetary policy, fiscal policy or both. It entails important legitimacy issues. **Gene Frieda** opined that QE makes safe assets less safe. Consequently, risk appetite has diminished. Is this lower risk appetite an issue in designing a portfolio? **Thomas Mayer** agreed that low risk appetite is a big problem. Last year, correlations across asset classes turned positive. The usual portfolio diversification did not work anymore. In response to Edwin Truman's question, he mentioned that the policies discussed might have been useful in preventing another Great Depression. However, given the current state of the economy, it is doubtful that these policies can now foster growth. This is where the report is not entirely convincing. Moreover, should we enter into another recession, helicopter money needs to be seriously considered as the tools that we have used so far might not be any longer effective. It is necessary to differentiate between the fiscal policy effect and the monetary policy effect in the general debate on helicopter money. This has not happened so far because central banks treat the issue as taboo.

According to **Alexander Swoboda**, there are international consequences of lowering interest rates. If the main channel of transmission is through the exchange rate, which even for the Eurozone seems to be the case, there is a problem of monetary policy coordination.

**Dirk Niepelt** drew attention to the recent discussion on the neo-Fisherian proposition, which contends that raising rates causes inflation to increase. Should central banks raise interest rates to get inflation up again?

**Gaston Gelos** pointed out that some banks in fact transmit negative deposit rates to their customers through higher fees. It would be interesting to see under which circumstances and to what degree banks are able to, de facto, pass on negative rate. **Shushil Wadhwani** mentioned that firms may postpone investment spending in response to negative rates. Negative rates can be perceived as an indication that central banks see the economic circumstances as worsening. Moreover, there must be a limit on how high the fees charged by banks to their customer can be. Ultimately, this will restrict the effectiveness of negative rates.

On communication, **Jean Boivin** replied that the expectation channel, and thus communication, is crucial. Communication alone, however, will not be able to reverse current developments. Moreover, it should spell out a contingency plan in case of another recession. With respect to helicopter money, he argued that there is nothing magical about it. It is more fiscal in nature than monetary. Another element is that policymakers should not limit their actions to fiscal policies because of Ricardian equivalence, although it might not be fully binding. A key question is how we achieve coordination between fiscal policy and monetary policy. In addition, communication also matters for fiscal authorities, which could implement a forward guidance communication strategy for fiscal policy. Finally, on negative rates, he agreed that the limit might be close.

# Lessons from policymakers

## Comments by the discussants

**Per Callesen,** *Danemarks Nationalbank*

One aspect that has been missing from the debate so far is whether low interest rates are really due to central bank action, or whether there is something more fundamental at work. In a world without central banks and with zero inflation, a situation in which desired savings are higher than desired investment would result in low interest rates. We cannot assume that interest rates would be much higher in the absence of central bank action. Other reasons behind low rates are deleveraging and adversity towards real risk.

Low interest rates seem to work also for the real economy, even if monetary policy is likely to face decreasing returns to scale as most interest rates have by now approached zero. The somehow disappointing pickup in demand growth is not evidence to the contrary. An analogy could be a car going uphill. You may press harder on the accelerator, yet still lose speed. The explanation is rather the difficulty of circumstances, not that the accelerator has stopped working. You will also not move faster by otherwise pushing the brakes, although you have to be well prepared for such a change when approaching the top of the hill.

Yet, there are some concerns that the report could address in greater detail. Asset prices are increasing in a way that might create bubbles. Moreover, there might be distortions related to productivity. Low rates allow companies that would otherwise exit the market to remain in business. It is uncertain what will happen once central banks increase rates again. With respect to helicopter money, it is vital to consider the micro issue and the macro issue. The micro issue is that the central bank would interfere with the microeconomic decision power of the fiscal authority by directly transferring money to citizens. In a macro context, it would be interesting to look at the difference between issuing money on the one hand, and sovereign debt at zero interest rates on the other hand. Regarding the proposal to raise the inflation target, in order to avoid hitting the lower bound in future deep crises, that bear costs and risks, much better for policymakers to better prevent such crises.

Denmark has had negative interest rates for almost four years, longer than anyone else. The Danish experience suggests that negative interest rates at current moderate levels work just like interest rates that are lower than very low interest rates. They spill over into money market rates as well as lending rates and deposit rates. The exchange rate channel appears to work. A technical challenge in the mortgage system has been to figure out how to handle a stream of payments from the creditor to the borrower. In practice, this has been managed by having an upfront redemption instead of a continuous payment. Negative rates also posed some challenges for the tax system.

Negative rates can potentially affect cash holdings. Commercial banks have not requested to substitute reserves with cash. It is costly to manage cash and to invest in its transportation, and it is unlikely that commercial banks will increase their cash holdings. Private banks have passed on negative rates to large institutional investors and non-financial companies. This is desirable as it is part of the monetary policy transmission mechanism, and they have not substituted into cash holdings, no doubt due the costs of that. So far, negative interest rates have not been pass on to retail depositors. The first-mover effect would probably

be substantial; it has prevented banks from passing on negative rates. Another reason is that banks no longer have the capacity to deal with the management of cash, which would require them to set up new facilities and re-open branches.

Another common concern with respect to negative rates is the profitability of the banking system. This does not seem to be an issue in Denmark. Last year, banks had the best year in terms of profits since the crisis, despite low interest rates. Higher fees, lower impairment charges and larger trading volumes have compensated for negative rates.

**Glenn Rudebusch,** *Federal Reserve Bank San Francisco*
The intense price pressures of the 1970s and 1980s were a transformational challenge for central banks. The ensuing Great Inflation and the painfully slow disinflation that followed indelibly shaped both the methods and mandates of monetary policy. Central banks were required to reinforce their policy tools and their institutional standing in order to be able to reduce inflation whenever necessary.

The resulting intense focus on defending inflation targets from upside risks did not position central banks well for their current predicament, when the credibility of inflation targets is at risk from below. During the Great Inflation, few imagined that, just a couple of decades later, monetary policymakers would encounter as difficult a challenge from the *opposite* direction, facing strong and seemingly intractable deflationary pressures. Indeed, few believed that inflation could persist below target in many countries for years on end. In large part, this lack of imagination reflected a general consensus that any central bank would have little difficulty producing higher inflation if necessary. For example, in the 1990s and early 2000s, Japan's persistent stagnation and deflation was blamed by many on a lack of central bank initiative, rather than a lack of monetary policy efficacy. Economists typically viewed the theoretical linkage from increases in the money supply to increases in the price level as providing a simple, ironclad, and even foolproof means of reflating the economy. Of course, as is evident in many countries, employing monetary policy to push up inflation has proved much harder in practice than in theory.

The Federal Reserve's response to the financial crisis and Great Recession included cutting the short-term policy interest rate to nearly zero in December 2008. However, the resulting cumulative reduction of just over 500 basis points was about the same magnitude of the policy rate reduction for the much milder recession in 2001. In the absence of a lower bound on nominal interest rates, the Fed likely would have pushed the funds rate substantially lower in the aftermath of the Great Recession.

The Fed used two additional tools to provide additional monetary policy stimulus and overcome the lower bound on nominal interest rates: forward policy guidance about the future path of the funds rate; and substantial purchases of government bonds, which greatly increased the size and duration of the Fed's portfolio. Each of these tools is often associated with one of the components of longer-term bond yields: forward funds rate guidance is assumed to lower the expectations component, while bond purchases lower the term premium. In fact, this separation is not very satisfactory. Credible forward guidance that the funds rate will be kept at low levels for longer than expected will push down the expectations component. But by curtailing the risks of a bad outcome, it is also

likely to reduce the risk premium. Similarly, the bond purchases undertaken for quantitative easing are also likely to send signals about the future path of the funds rate.

One way to gauge the effect of the Fed's forward guidance about the future policy rate is to examine the evolution of funds rate projections in financial markets. Taking risk-neutral readings in fed funds and Eurodollar futures markets as reasonable indicators of interest rate predictions, financial market participants appeared to expect a fairly steep upward funds rate trajectory in the years just after the recession ended. But later on, from 2011 through 2013, this expectation for early lift-off was greatly tempered. An important reason for this flattening of market-implied funds rate expectations was the Fed's forward guidance. For example, at the August 2011 meeting, the Federal Open Market Committee (FOMC) noted that economic conditions "are likely to warrant exceptionally low levels of the federal funds rate at least through mid-2013". Subsequently, this was extended through late 2014, then through mid-2015, and eventually to depend explicitly on economic conditions. These instances of forward guidance were correlated with a dramatic flattening of the expected future path of the funds rate. Indeed, it was only after the introduction of this forward guidance that the two-year rate was definitively pushed down to near zero.

To provide additional monetary policy stimulus, the FOMC purchased large amounts of government bonds in the secondary market. The Fed's securities holdings increased by an order of magnitude – from $500 billion to almost $4.5 trillion or, relative to nominal GDP, from 5% to 25%. The Fed's portfolio also took on a longer duration. There is substantial empirical evidence showing the impact of longer-term bond purchases by the Fed and other central banks had on financial markets. The so-called 'taper tantrum' of 2013 provides a particularly salient example. The market's surprise at the news that the Fed might curtail future bond purchases was enough to push up 10-year Treasury yields by more than a percentage point, which indicates the sensitivity of longer-term yields to news about Fed purchases.

Although the Fed did not push the short-term policy rate below zero during this episode, negative interest rates could be an option in the future under severely adverse conditions. However, the effectiveness of negative interest rates depends crucially on the specific structure of financial markets and institutions, so what works in one country may not have similar effects in another. Also, cuts in the policy rate are most effective when they are expected to be long-lasting rather than temporary. That is, lowering the policy rate to negative 50 basis points and indicating that it is likely to persist could be a significant disincentive to saving. Unfortunately, that forward guidance may also give savers an incentive to invest in, for example, cash deposit facilities.

Finally, an important issue for future research is how to avoid or mitigate the effects of the lower bound in the longer run. The tools we have available for raising the real equilibrium rate of interest, say, through fiscal actions, appear weak. But raising the perceived inflation target is not straightforward, as these perceptions appear heavily anchored by experience.

**Andréa M.** *Maechler, Swiss National Bank*
This timely report discusses different dimensions of a very important subject. Three points merit detailed comments. First comes the question of how to assess the effectiveness of monetary policy. The second point is the question of what the liquidity trap concept means for monetary policy in the context of a small and open economy with an overvalued currency, which has traditionally been used as safe haven. The third point is the report's proposal to raise central banks' inflation targets.

With regards to the first point, different factors are responsible for the secular decline in global interest rates. These factors include, in particular, the severity of the last global financial crisis as well as various longer-term structural developments, such as population ageing and falling productivity growth in some important advanced economies. Hence, a focus on monetary policy alone, as advocated by the report, is unlikely to produce sustainable solutions to the challenges of the low interest rate environment. Monetary policy has limits that must be recognised. Otherwise there is a risk that monetary policy will be overburdened.

On the second point, it must be stressed that Switzerland has not experienced a liquidity trap in the strict Keynesian sense. In particular, bank lending is not impaired and the SNB's monetary policy is not focused on stimulating lending growth. Instead, the Swiss economy is faced with an overvalued exchange rate, which weighs down on price inflation. Since early 2015, the SNB's monetary policy has been based on two elements: a negative interest rate on sight deposit balances that reduces the attractiveness of Swiss franc-denominated investments, and the SNB's willingness to intervene in foreign exchange markets as necessary.

While it could lower the negative interest rate further, the SNB has gone comparatively far by reducing the rate to –0.75%. The report's proposal to reduce the SNB's deposit rate to –2.25% for one year in order to 'kick-start' the economy would not be consistent with the SNB's aim to counter excessive upward pressure on the Swiss franc exchange rate. The SNB's negative interest rate has been transmitted to money and capital markets. It has been effective in reducing the attractiveness of Swiss franc-denominated investments. At the same time, it limits risks, such as a sharp rise in the demand for cash and an undue distortion of savings and investment decisions.

The report rightly notes that low interest rates may increase risks to financial stability. To limit the burden that the negative interest rate places on bank profitability, the SNB has granted generous exemptions from its application. In addition, to mitigate imbalances in the mortgage and real estate markets, Switzerland has implemented macroprudential measures, including a countercyclical capital buffer on banks' capital.

Regarding the final point, one must be sceptical about the idea of raising central banks' inflation targets. The SNB does not have an inflation target. Instead, it equates price stability with a rise in consumer prices of less than 2% per annum over the medium term. The SNB has consistently met its price stability objective. It enjoys a high degree of credibility. For Switzerland, higher average inflation is not commensurate with price stability. Raising the target range for price stability would not improve the Swiss economy's ability to absorb shocks, but would risk undermining the SNB's credibility.

**Zhang Tao,** *People's Bank of China*

Zhang Tao addressed two related issues: financial stability and international coordination. In the past, central banks' mandates largely focused on price stability although some mandates included other objectives, such as full employment or targets related to the balance of payment. Recently, many central banks have taken up financial stability concerns. This presents central banks with a trade-off between inflation and financial stability. Employing negative interest rates and QE for too long may distort asset prices, lower risk awareness and accelerate bank dis-intermediation. Ultimately, this could jeopardise financial stability. Another issue related to unconventional monetary policies is international coordination. In fact, this issue is not new. In an increasingly globalised world, even conventional policies can create issues of spillovers and spillbacks. Research suggests that there are significant spillover effects through the portfolio rebalancing channel, the liquidity channel and the signalling channel. These effects could be different for conventional and unconventional monetary policies, however. The report could benefit from discussing these potential differences.

China has not yet implemented negative interest rates. China is not facing a liquidity trap, but rather liquidity rigidity, meaning that the transmission of the interest rate is not flexible. As a result, monetary policy has been conducted through a combination of monetary aggregates and interest rates. Recently, the People's Bank of China has launched purchase facilities that are similar to the ones used by the Fed in the US. The purpose is to ensure that monetary policy can be useful in countering cycles on the one hand and providing support for structural reforms on the other hand. On the Chinese monetary policy stance, the monetary aggregate has remained stable during recent years. Earlier this year, there was a stable increase in supply, including in bank lending. This has led markets to speculate that the monetary policy stance will become more expansionary. This is not the case, however. The increase in money supply reflects seasonal fluctuations and the need to stabilise stock markets. These have stabilised now, implying that money supply is coming back to its normal level. Furthermore, the People's Bank of China has removed ceilings on deposit rates last year as a final step in its interest rate liberalisation programme. This has helped to thwart cyclical pressures.

For the rest of the year 2016, monetary policy will remain unchanged. It will concentrate on supporting sustainable growth and providing accommodation for the structural reforms that aim at transforming China from an export-based economy to a more consumption driven economy. Reforms are key for the deleveraging of the economy. High levels of debt have recently drawn much attention. In fact, household and government debt levels are low compared to corporate sector debt levels. This raises issues of distributional effects and efficiency. The reforms are geared towards tackling these issues. In this context, it is important to improve the social safety net to let people save less and spend more. Finally, the currency reform must be completed. It aims at increasing market flexibility and anchoring expectations.

## General discussion

**Charles Wyplosz** was intrigued that central bankers argued that QE does not work as effectively as perceived. The literature on QE, largely produced by central banks, has argued that QE is effective. Following up on this remark, **Gareth Ramsey** noted that central banks have always emphasised that QE was more uncertain than conventional policies. In addition, it might well be state-contingent in terms of its effect. Central bankers are not necessarily opposed to asset purchases, but they might be concerned about overburdening monetary policy. The report went quite far in asking monetary policy to address a wide range of issues without stressing enough the importance of understanding the structural factors driving current economic conditions.

**Katrin Asssenmacher** asked the authors whether they have a view on the ranking of the various unconventional policies. Different countries have taken different approaches, often depending on the institutional and legal set-up. A more differentiated analysis of which instrument should be used in which situation could add to the report's value. **Jan Toth** asked if it would not be better to target medium-term rates instead of conducting QE because it does not affect the central bank's balance sheet.

**Edwin Truman** understood from the discussion that unconventional monetary policy was essentially an exchange rate policy in Switzerland. Why did the SNB not use unconventional monetary policy to support the domestic economy rather than manipulating the exchange rate? **Alexander Swoboda** responded that, in a small open economy, monetary policy is exchange rate policy. That is what the Mundell-Fleming model and perfect capital mobility tell us. **Vit Bárta** confirmed that in the Czech Republic, unconventional policies have promoted exchange rate depreciation and succeeded in boosting the economy. He encouraged the authors to study the Czech experience. **Avinash Persaud** concluded that it might be the case that exchange rate policy is hiding behind unconventional tools. If so, this would constitute a political economy issue.

**Ugo Panizza** followed up on remarks that the inflation target should not be increased, given that we do not know how to reach it. If this were true, we should not conduct monetary policy with an inflation targeting framework as it relies on the idea that the target can be reached. **Jacques Delpla** wondered what we should do with central bankers who fail and miss their mandate year after year. Several years after the crisis, we are still in deflation. Central bank independence raises the question of who is guarding the guardians. **Avinash Persaud** wondered who is responsible for the quality as opposed to the quantity of lending. Increasingly, there are highly leveraged short-term investments, reflecting currently low interest rates.

In response to these comments, **Per Callesen** reaffirmed that monetary policy works. Importantly, however, there might be decreasing returns. On the debate on exchange rate policy in small open economies, he noted that Denmark has anchored its exchange rate for 35 years. Formally, Denmark is manipulating its exchange rate every day because it is effectively a member of the Eurozone. **Glenn Rudebusch** replied to the point made by Charles Wyplosz on the effectiveness of QE. Many of the studies on the effectiveness of QE are event studies that look at the financial market impact. There is less clarity about the real-term effects of

QE. With respect to setting long-term interest rates, he mentioned that it is just a matter of setting the price or quantity. Setting the price implies losing control over quantity and the size of the balance sheet.

**Andréa M. Maechler** noted that there are two angles of Swiss monetary policy. First, it reacts to global spillovers in the form of safe haven inflows. Second, there is a real economy story behind it. Switzerland has historically had a current account surplus. These savings were typically invested abroad. Since 2007, however, savings have returned to Switzerland or just not been re-invested abroad. This is a direct result of the crisis. The negative interest rate has restored the historical interest rate differential and encouraged investment abroad. This is why the negative interest rate works for the Swiss monetary policy framework and is not an exchange rate manipulation. **Zhang Tao** added that in a small open economy, there is a trade-off between independent monetary policy and exchange rate policy. Facing this challenge, different small open economies have chosen different paths.

**Patrick Honohan** summarised the authors' response. The report starts with the message that inflation is a monetary phenomenon. Central banks operate in financial markets to raise or lower financing costs, and they can continue to do so. The authors narrowed the scope of the report to discuss just what central banks can do. Implementing at the same time other policies, such as fiscal policy and structural policies, would get the economy moving in a better way and get inflation up to the target. By not discussing these policies, the report accepts that the policy mix implicitly recommended is not optimal, but it is what central banks can do. The central bank's mandate is not conditional on what others do, and central banks cannot dodge their responsibility in this regard.

Although the report argues that monetary policy can be effective at the zero lower bound, it accepts that there are some concerns to be addressed. Comprehensive communication is needed to challenge the money illusion story. A key point of the report is that a deep temporary cut ensures that interest rates can return positive faster. This might be different in certain economies, such as Switzerland, where negative rates aim at countering safe haven inflows. Unconventional monetary policies might face diminishing marginal effectiveness on inflation and employment. The evidence is not clear. If the effectiveness is diminishing, central banks may have to do more.

An important question from a political economy point of view is whether central banks have the legitimacy to act on this scale. Does the political economy equilibrium have to be re-negotiated? At present, central banks have very clear mandates. We could start to open a dialogue about a future mandate where the political economy equilibrium is slightly different but, for the moment, central banks cannot shy away. The questions of whether there is an unacceptable fiscal aspect to it and whether there are redistribution issues have to be analysed. Equity purchases are an unconventional area for central banks. There are no adequate, historical precedents. Helicopter money is in the same territory.

Finally, on overburdening central banks, the authors argued that central banks cannot walk away from their responsibility to deal with inflation and inflation expectations. Some comments suggest that there is a view out there that central banks do not have to follow an inflation target. They can allow inflation drift lower, even into negative territory. This is not an acceptable position for central banks.

# Appendix: The model used for simulations

The model's first equation is a standard Taylor rule with the addition of a lower bound on the interest rate:

$$i_t = max[i^{LB}{}_t, \ i^{TR}{}_t], \tag{8.1}$$

where $i^{TR}$ is given by equation

$$i^{TR}{}_t = r^* + \pi^{\#}{}_t + 0.5 \ (\pi^{\#}{}_t - \pi^*) - 2.0 u_t \tag{8.2}$$

and $i^{LB}$ is the lower bound. We will sometimes set $i^{LB}{}_t$ at approximately zero, and sometimes at a negative level.[88] $r^*$ is the equilibrium real interest rate; $\pi^{\#}$ is the 4-quarter moving average of inflation; $\pi^*$ is the inflation target; and $u$ is the unemployment gap (actual unemployment minus the natural rate).

The second equation is a dynamic Phillips curve:

$$\pi_t = \pi^* - 0.5 u^{\#}{}_{t-1} + \eta_t , \tag{8.3}$$

where $u^{\#}$ is the 4-quarter moving average of the unemployment gap. Empirical work suggests this lag structure is realistic (e.g. Ball, 2015). $\eta$ is a price or supply shock.

The final equation is a dynamic IS equation:

$$u_t = 0.95 u_{t-1} + 0.05(i^{\#}{}_{t-1} - \pi^{\#}{}_{t-1} - r^*) + \varepsilon_t , \tag{8.4}$$

where $i^{\#}$ is the 4-quarter moving average of the nominal interest rate. $\varepsilon$ is an unemployment or demand shock. This equation is a simple version of the IS equations estimated by Rudebusch and Svensson (1999) and Laubach and Williams (2000), except with unemployment substituted for output based on an implicit Okun's Law. Our specification implies that a one percentage point rise in the real interest rate over the previous four quarters raises unemployment by 0.05 points (equivalent to a decrease of 0.1% in output). Because of the lagged unemployment term, if the interest rate remains elevated indefinitely, the effect on unemployment grows to 1.0 percentage point. The behaviour of the model is presumably sensitive to the coefficients in equation (8.4), and there is less consensus about reasonable values for these parameters than for those of the Taylor Rule and Phillips curve.

---

[88] Our historical simulations assume that the lower bound is the effective federal funds rate during the period that the Fed set its target as a range from 0% to 0.25%.

To model the effect of QE, we modify the IS curve to include both short-term and long-term interest rates:

$$u_t = 0.95u_{t-1} + 0.025(i^{\#}_{t-1} - \pi^{\#}_{t-1} - r^*) + 0.10(x^{\#}_{t-1} - \pi^L_{t-1} - r^* - \tau^*) + \varepsilon_t, \quad (8.4')$$

where $x$ is the long-term interest rate (bond yield), $\pi^L$ is long-term expected inflation, and $\tau^*$ is the average term premium in bond yields.

$$x_t = 0.25i_t + 0.75(r^* + \pi^*) + \tau_t \quad (8.5)$$

$$\pi^L_t = 0.25\pi^{\#}_t + 0.75\pi^* \quad (8.6)$$

Here the long-term rate responds partially to the short-term rate and partially to the steady-state rate. Similarly, the long-term inflation expectation responds partially to current inflation and partially to target inflation. $\tau$ is a term premium in the long-term rate. We choose the coefficients in equations (8.4'), (8.5), and (8.6) to satisfy the following criteria: (1) equation (8.4') reduces to equation (8.4) when the term premium equals its average value; (2) the effect of the short rate on the long rate is close to its empirically estimated value (Chung et al. 2011; Kiley 2014); and (3) the IS-curve effect of a reduction in the long rate while holding the short rate constant is half of the effect of the same long-rate reduction achieved by cutting the short rate (Chen et al. 2012; Kiley, 2014).

Substituting equations (8.5) and (8.6) into equation (8.4') yields

$$u_t = 0.95u_{t-1} + 0.05(i^{\#}_{t-1} - \pi^{\#}_{t-1} - r^*) + 0.10(\tau^{\#}_{t-1} - \tau^*) + \varepsilon_t, \quad (8.4'')$$

We model the effect of QE by a change in the term premium. In particular, for the simulation of the Great Recession with no QE, we increase the term premium starting in 2009:Q1 by 50 basis points and rising in steps to 125 basis points in 2013:Q1 through the end of the simulation, based on the analysis of Engen et al. (2015).

The data used in the simulations are from Haver Analytics and the Congressional Budget Office (CBO). They are the effective federal funds rate, the 10-year Treasury yield, the rate of change of the personal consumption expenditures deflator excluding food and energy, and the civilian unemployment rate minus the CBO estimate of the natural rate of unemployment.

# References

Agarwal, R. and M.S. Kimball (2015), "Breaking Through the Zero Lower Bound", IMF Working Paper No. 15/224.

Akerlof, G. A., W.T. Dickens and G.L. Perry (1996), "The Macroeconomics of Low Inflation", *Brookings Papers on Economic Activity* 1: 1–59.

Assenmacher-Wesche, K. and S. Gerlach (2010), "Monetary policy and financial imbalances: facts and fiction", *Economic Policy* 25: 437-482.

Bagnall, J., D. Bounie, K. P. Huynh, A. Kosse, T. Schmidt, S. Schuh and H. Stix (2014), "Consumer cash usage: a cross-country comparison with payment diary survey data", ECB Working Paper No. 1685.

Ball, L. (2013), "The Case for Four Percent Inflation", *Central Bank Review* 13: 17-31.

Bank for International Settlements (2016), 86th Annual Report.

Ball, L. (2014), "Long-Term Damage from the Great Recession", NBER Working Paper No. 20185.

Ball, L. (2015), "Comment on "Inflation and activity" by Olivier Blanchard, Eugenio Cerutti and Lawrence Summers", *ECB Forum on Central Banking*, pp. 47-52.

Bank of Canada (2015), "Forward Guidance at the Effective Lower Bound: International Experience", Bank of Canada Staff Discussion Paper 2015-15.

Bank of England (2014a), "The Economics of Digital Currencies", *Quarterly Bulletin* Q3: 1-11.

Bank of England (2014b), *Inflation Report*, November.

Bank of England (2015), *Financial Stability Report*, July.

Bank of Japan (2012), *Annual Review*.

Bank of Japan (2016), "Outlook for Economic Activity and Prices", April.

Bank of Japan (various dates), Statements on Monetary Policy.

Bean, C., C. Broda, T. Ito and R. Kroszner (2015), *Low for Long? Causes and Consequences of Persistently Low Interest Rates*, Geneva Reports on the World Economy 17, ICMB and CEPR.

Bech, M. and A. Malhozov (2016), "How have central banks implemented negative policy rates?", *BIS Quarterly Review*, March.

Benigno, P. and L.A. Ricci (2011), "The Inflation-Output Trade-Off with Downward Wage Rigidities", *American Economic Review* 101(4): 1436-1466.

Bennett, B., D. Canover, S. O'Brian and R. Advincula (2014), "Cash Continues to Play and Key Role in Consumer Spending: Evidence from the Diary of Consumer Payment Choice", memo, Cash Product Office of the Federal Reserve System.

Bentow, D. (2015), "Fangernes dilemma, Las Vegas og Draghis bazooka: Forstå spillet om kronen", Finanswatch.dk, 6 February.

Bernanke, B.S. (2000), "Japanese Monetary Policy: A Case of Self-Induced Paralysis?", in A. Posen and R. Mikitani (eds), *Japan's Financial Crisis and Its Parallels to US Experience*, Special Report 13, Washington, DC: Institute for International Economics, pp. 149–166.

Bernanke, B.S. (2010), Testimony before the Joint Economic Committee of Congress, 14 April.

Bernanke, B.S. (2012), "Monetary Policy since the Onset of the Crisis", Board of Governors of the Federal Reserve System at the Federal Reserve Bank of Kansas City Economic Symposium Jackson Hole, Wyoming.

Bernanke, Ben S. (2015), "Monetary Policy in the Future", speech at the Brookings Institution, Washington, DC, 15 April (available at www.brookings.edu/blogs/ben-bernanke).

Betalingsraadet (2013), "Rapport om Nye Betalingsloesninger", Copenhangen: Danmarks Nationalbank.

Blanchard, O. (2016) "The US Phillips Curve: Back to the 60s?", Policy Brief 16-1, Peterson Institute for International Economics, Washington, DC.

Blanchard, O., G. Dell'Ariccia, and P. Mauro (2010), "Rethinking Macroeconomic Policy", *Journal of Money, Credit and Banking* 42(s1): 199-215.

Blanchard, O., E. Cerutti and L. Summers (2015), "Inflation and Activity: Two Explorations and their Monetary Policy Implications", ECB Forum on Central Banking, pp 25-46.

Blattner, T.S. and E. Margaritov (2010), "Towards a robust monetary policy rule for the euro area", ECB Working Paper NO. 1210.

Borio, C. and H. Zhu (2012), "Capital regulation, risk-taking and monetary policy: a missing link in the transmission mechanism?", *Journal of Financial Stability* 8(4): 236-251.

Borio, C., L. Gambercorta and B. Hofmann (2015a), "The influence of monetary policy on bank profitability", BIS Working Paper No. 514.

Borio, C., M. Erdem, A. Filardo and B. Hofmann (2015b), "The costs of deflations: a historical perspective", *BIS Quarterly Review,* March.

Borio, C., P. Disyatat and A. Zabai (2016), "Helicopter money: The illusion of a free lunch", VoxEU.org, 24 May (www.voxeu.org/article/helicopter-money-illusion-free-lunch).

Buiter, W.H. (2007), "Is Numérairology the Future of Monetary Economics? Unbundling Numéraire and Medium of Exchange through a Virtual Currency with a Shadow Exchange Rate", *Open Economies Review* 18: 127-156.

Buiter, W.H. (2009), "Negative Nominal Interest Rates: Three Ways to Overcome the Zero Lower Bound", *North American Journal of Economics and Finance* 20(3): 213-238.

Buiter, W.H. (2014), "The Simple Analytics of Helicopter Money: Why It Works – Always", *Economics: The Open-Access, Open Assessment E-Journal* 8:2014-28 .

Burke, C., S. Hilton, R. Judson, K. Lewis, and S. Skeie (2010), "Reducing the IOER Rate: An Analysis of Options", FOMC Note, 5 August.

Caballero, R.J. and E. Farhi (2016), "The Safety Trap", NBER Working Paper No. 19927.

Campbell, J.R., C.L. Evans, J.D.M. Fisher and A. Justiniano (2012), "Macroeconomic Effects of Federal Reserve Forward Guidance", *Brookings Papers on Economic Activity* 44(1): 1-80.

Carpenter, S., S. Demiralp and J. Eisenschmidt (2013), "The Effectiveness of the Non-Standard Policy Measures during the Financial Crises The Experiences of the Federal Reserve and the European Central Bank", ECB Working Paper No. 1562.

Carroll C.D., M. Otsuka and J. Slacalek (2011), "How Large Are Housing and Financial Wealth Effects? A New Approach", *Journal of Money, Credit and Banking* 41(1): 55-79.

Cecchetti, S. G. and K.L. Schoenholtz (2016), "How Low Can They Go?", commentary on *Money&Banking*, 29 Februrary (www.moneyandbanking.com).

Chen, H., V. Curdia and A. Ferrero (2012), "The Macroeconomic Effects of Large-Scale Asset Purchase Programs", Working Paper 2012-22, Federal Reserve Bank of San Francisco.

Chodorow-Reich, G. (2014), "Effects of Unconventional Monetary Policy on Financial Institutions", *Brookings Papers on Economic Activity* (Spring): 155-204.

Christensen, J.H.E. and S. Krogstrup (2016), "Transmission of Quantitative Easing: The Role of Central Bank Reserves", FRBSF Working paper 2014-18.

Christensen, J.H.E., J.A. Lopez and G.D. Rudebusch (2015), "A Probability-based Stress Test of Federal Reserve Assets and Income", *Journal of Monetary Economics* 73: 26-43.

Chung, H., J.-P. Laforte, D. Reifschneider and J.C. Williams (2011), "Have We Underestimated the Likelihood and Severity of Zero Lower Bound Events?", Working Paper 2011-01, Federal Reserve Bank of San Francisco.

Churm, R., M. Joyce, G. Kapetanios, and K. Theodoridis (2015), "Unconventional Monetary Policies and the Macroeconomy: The Impact of the United Kingdom's QE2 and Funding for Lending Scheme", Bank of England Staff Working Paper 542.

Claessens, S., N. Coleman and M. Donnelly (2016), "'Low for long' interest rates and net interest margins of banks in Advanced Foreign Economies", IFDP Notes, Federal Reserve Board, 11 April.

Coenen, G.A. Orphanides, and V. Wieland (2004), "Price Stability and Monetary Policy Effectiveness When Nominal Interest Rates Are Bounded at Zero", Advances in Macroeconomics 4(1): 1–23.

Coenen, G. and A. Warne (2014), "Risks to Price Stability, the Zero Lower Bound, and Forward Guidance: A Real-Time Assessment", *International Journal of Central Banking*, June.

Coeuré, B. (2016a), "From challenges to opportunities: rebooting the European financial sector", Keynote speech at Süddeutsche Zeitung Finance Day 2016, Frankfurt am Main, 2 March.

Coeuré, B. (2016), "Assessing the implications of negative interest rates", speech at the Yale Financial Crisis Forum, Yale School of Management, New Haven, 28 July.

Committee on Payments and Market Infrastructures (2015), *Digital Currencies*, November.

Côté, A. (2014), "Inflation Targeting in the Post-Crisis Era", Speech to the Calgary CFA Society, Calgary, Alberta, 18 November.

Craig, B.R. and V. Dinger (2011), "The Duration of Bank Retail Interest Rates", Working Papers 88, Institute of Empirical Economic Research.

Danmarks Nationalbank (2015), "Negative interest rates and their impact on credit insitutions' earnings", *Financial Stability*, 1st Half 2015.

Danmarks Nationalbank (2016), *Monetary Review*, 1st Quarter 2016.

Danthine, J.-P. (2016), "The Interest Rate Unbound?", paper presented at the Brookings Institution Conference on Negative Interest Rates, 6 June.

Darracq-Paries, M. and R. De Santis (2013), "A Non-Standard Monetary Policy Shock: The ECB's 3-Year LTROs and the Shift in Credit Supply", ECB Working Paper 1508.

De Michelis, A. and M. Iacoviello (2016), "Raising an Inflation Target: The Japanese Experience with Abenomics", International Finance Discussion Papers No. 1168, Board of Governors of the Federal Reserve System, Washington, DC.

Del Negro, M., M. Giannoni, and C. Patterson (2012), "The Forward Guidance Puzzle", Federal Reserve Bank of New York Staff Report No. 574 (revised December 2015).

Dixit, A.K. (1989), "Entry and Exit Decisions under Uncertainty", *Journal of Political Economy* 97(3): 620-38.

Draghi, M. (2015), "Monetary Policy: Past, Present and Future", speech at the Frankfurt European Banking Congress (www.ecb.europa.eu/press/key/date/2015/html/sp151120.en.html).

Eggertsson, G.B. and M. Woodford (2003), "The Zero Bound on Interest Rates and Optimal Monetary Policy", *Brookings Papers on Economic Activity* 2003(1): 139-233.

Engen E.M., T.T. Laubach and D. Reifschneider (2015), "The Macroeconomic Effects of the Federal Reserve's Unconventional Monetary Policies", Finance and Economics Discussion Series 2015-005, Board of Governors of the Federal Reserve System, Washington, DC.

European Central Bank (2011), "The Use of Euro Banknotes – Results of Two Surveys Among Households and Firms", *Monthly Bulletin* (April): 79-90.

European Central Bank (2014), "The ECB's Forward Guidance", Monthly Bulletin 2014(4): 65-73.

European Central Bank (2015), "The impact of negative short-term rates on the money market fund industry", *Monthly Bulletin* 5, Box 5.

European Central Bank (2016), *Monthly Bulletin*, March.

Farmer, R. and P. Zabczyk (2016), "The Theory of Unconventional Monetary Policy", NBER Working Paper No. 22135.

Feldstein, M. (1997), "The Costs and Benefits of Going from Low Inflation to Price Stability", in C. Romer and D. Romer (eds), Reducing Inflation: Motivation and Strategy, NBER Studies in Business Cycles, vol. 30. Chicago: University of Chicago Press.

Filardo, A. and B. Hofmann (2014), "Forward guidance at the zero lower bound", BIS Quarterly Review, March.

Fischer, S. (2016), "Monetary Policy, Financial Stability, and the Zero Lower Bound". speech given at the Annual Meeting of the American Economic Association, San Francisco, 3 January.

Friedman, B.M. (2014), "Has the Financial Crisis Permanently Changed the Practice of Monetary Policy? Has It Changed the Theory of Monetary Policy?" NBER Working Paper No. 20128 (also in *The Manchester School* 83(S1): 5–19, 2015).

Friedman, M. (1969) *The Optimal Quantity of Money and Other Essays*, Chicago: Aldine.

Gagnon, J. (2016), "Quantitative Easing: An Underappreciated Success", PIIE Policy Brief 16-4, Washington, DC.

Gagnon, J. and M. Hinterschweiger (2013), "Responses of Central Banks in Advanced Economies to the Global Financial Crisis", in C. Rhee and A. Posen (eds), *Responding to Financial Crisis: Lessons from Asia Then, the United States and Europe Now*, Washington, DC: Peterson Institute for International Economics and Asian Development Bank.

Gagnon, J.E. and B. Sack (2014), "Monetary Policy with Abundant Liquidity: A New Operating Framework for the Federal Reserve", PIIE Policy Brief 14-4, Washington, DC.

Galí, J. (2008), *Monetary Policy, Inflation and the Business Cycle: An Introduction to the New Keynesian Framework*, Princeton, NJ: Princeton University Press.

García, J.A. and T. Werner (2010), "Inflation Risks and Inflation Risk Premia", ECB Working Paper 1162.

Goldstein, M. (2016), *Banking's Final Exam: Stress Testing and Bank Capital Reform*, Washington, DC: PIIE Press, forthcoming.

Gerlach, P., P. Hördahl and R. Moessner (2011), "Inflation expectations and the great recession", *BIS Quarterly Review*, Bank for International Settlements, March.

Goodfriend, M. (2014), "The Relevance of Federal Reserve Surplus Capital for Current Policy", speech at the Shadow Open Market Committee Symposium, New York, 14 March.

Goodhart, C. and D. Lu (2003), *Intervention to Save Hong Kong*, Oxford: Oxford University Press.

Greenspan, A. (2001), "Transparency in Monetary Policy", speech at the Federal Reserve Bank of St. Louis (www.federalreserve.gov/boarddocs/speeches/2001/20011011/default.htm).

Greenwood, R. (2005), "Short- and Long-term Demand Curves for Stocks: Theory and Evidence on the Dynamics of Arbitrage", *Journal of Financial Economics* 75(3): 607-649.

Grisse, C., S. Krogstrup and S. Schumacher (2016), "Lower bound beliefs and long-term interest rates", manuscript, Swiss National Bank.

Hofmann, B. and P. Mizen (2004), "Interest Rate Pass-Through and Monetary Transmission: Evidence from Individual Financial Institutions' Retail Rates", *Economica* 71: 99–123.

Huizinga, J. (1993), "Inflation Uncertainty, Relative Price Uncertainty, and Investment in U.S. Manufacturing", *Journal of Money, Credit, and Banking* 25(3), 521–549.

Humphrey, D. (2010), "Retail payments: New contributions, empirical results, and unanswered questions", *Journal of Banking and Finance* 34.

Humphrey, D. (2015), "Negative Interest Rates and the Demand for Cash", Florida State University.

Ihrig, J., M. Marazzi, and A. Rothenberg (2006), "Exchange Rate Pass-Through in the G-7 Countries", International Finance Discussion Papers No. 851, Board of Governors of the Federal Reserve System, Washington, DC.

International Monetary Fund (2016), "Germany: Financial Sector Assessment Program-Financial System Stability Assessment", Washington DC (www.imf.org/external/pubs/cat/longres.aspx?sk=44013.0).

Ireland, P.N. (2009), "On the Welfare Cost of Inflation and the Recent Behavior of Money Demand", *American Economic Review* 99:3, 1040–1052.

James, H. (2015), "Dual Currencies", presentation at the CEPR, Imperial College and SNB conference "Removing the Zero Lower Bound On Interest Rates", London, 18 May.

*The Japan Times* (2012), "Abe pledges to make Bank of Japan buy bonds", 19 November.

Keynes, J.M. (1936), The General Theory of Employment, Interest, and Money (available at http://cas.umkc.edu/economics/people/facultypages/kregel/courses/econ645/winter2011/generaltheory.pdf).

Kiley M.T. (2014), "The aggregate demand effects of short- and long-term interest rates", *International Journal of Central Banking* 10(4): 69-104.

Kimball, M. (2016), "Enabling Deeper Negative Rates by Managing the Side Effects of a Zero Paper Currency Interest Rate", blog post (http://blog.supplysideliberal.com/post/145566511667/enabling-deeper-negative-rates-by-managing-the)

Kitsul, Y. and J.H. Wright (2013), "The Economics of Options-Implied Inflation Probability Density Functions", *Journal of Financial Economics* 110(3): 696-711.

Krishnamurthy, A. and A. Vissing-Jorgensen (2011), "The Effects of Quantitative Easing on Interest Rates", *Brookings Papers on Economic Activity* (Fall): 3–43.

Krugman, P. (1998), "It's Baaack! Japan's Slump and the Return of the Liquidity Trap", *Brookings Papers on Economic Activity* 1998:2, 137–187.

Kumhof, M. and J. Barrdear (2016), "The macroeconomics of central bank-issued digital currency", paper presented at the 2016 ASSA Conference, San Francisco.

Lachman, D. (2016), "Quantitative Easing's Chickens Comping Home to Roost", commentary, Manhattan Institute for Policy Research economics portal.

Laubach, T. and J. Williams (2015), "Measuring the Natural Rate of Interest Redux", Working Paper 2015-16, Federal Reserve Bank of San Francisco.

Lemke, W., M. Rostagno and T. Vlassopoulos (2016), "NLB: Negative (No) Lower Bound policy as an efficient monetary policy instrument", manuscript.

Liltoft Andreasen, B., P. Lassenius Kramp and A. Kuchler (2012), "The Banks' Interest Rates", *Danmarks Nationalbank Monetary Review*, 4th Quarter 2012, Part 1.

Lucas, R.E. (2000), "Inflation and Welfare", *Econometrica* 68(2): 247-274.

McAndrews, J. (2015), "Negative Nominal Central Bank Policy Rates: Where Is the Lower Bound?", Remarks at the University of Wisconsin, 8 May (www.ny.frb.org/newsevents/speeches/2015/mca150508.html).

Modigliani, F. and R.A. Cohn (1979), "Inflation, Rational Valuation and the Market", *Financial Analysts Journal* 35: 24-44

Moessner, R., D.-J. Jansen and J. de Haan (2015), "Communication about future policy rates in theory and practice: a survey", DNB Working Papers 475.

Nakamura, E., J. Steinsson, D. Villar and P. Sun (2016), "The Elusive Costs of Inflation: Price Dispersion during the U.S. Great Inflation", mimeo, Columbia University.

Neely, C. (2012), "The Large-Scale Asset Purchases Had Large International Effects", Working Paper 2010-018D, Federal Reserve Bank of St. Louis.

Nishimura, K.G. (2016), "Trois Changements 'Sismiques' dans l'Économie Mondiale et leurs Enjeux de Politique Économique", *Revue d'Économie Financière* 121: 131-144.

Norges Bank (2014), "Costs in the Norwegian payment system", Norges Bank Papers No. 5.

OECD (2016), *Economic Outlook 2016*, Issue 1.

Orphanides, A. (2004), "Monetary policy in deflation: the liquidity trap in history and practice", *North American Journal of Economics and Finance* 15: 101–124.

Perli, R., A. Laperriere and M. Turner (2016), "Negative Interest Rates or Safe Haven Flows: Which Matters More for Currencies?" Cornerstone Macro Economics, Policy, Strategy and Technicals Note, 18 April.

Petajisto, A. (2009), "Why Do Demand Curves for Stocks Slope Down?", *Journal of Financial and Quantitative Analysis* 44(5): 1013-1044.

Phelps, E.S. (1973), "Inflation in the Theory of Public Finance", *Scandinavian Journal of Economics* 75: 67-82.

Posen, A.S. (1998), *Restoring Japan's Economic Growth*, Washington, DC: Institute for International Economics.

Rodríguez Palenzuela, D., G. Camba-Méndez and J. Ángel García (2003), "Relevant Economic Issues Concerning the Optimal Rate of Inflation", ECB Working Paper 278.

Rogers, J., C. Scotti, and J. Wright (2014), "Evaluating Asset-Market Effects of Unconventional Monetary Policy: A Cross-Country Comparison", International Finance Discussion Paper 1101, Board of Governors of the Federal Reserve System.

Rogoff, K. (1985), "The Optimal Degree of Commitment to an Intermediate Monetary Target", *The Quarterly Journal of Economics* 100(4): 1169-1189.

Rogoff, K. (2014), "Costs and Benefits to Phasing Out Paper Currency", NBER Working Paper No. 20126.

Romer, C.D. (1992), "What Ended the Great Depression?", *Journal of Economic History* 52: 757–784.

Romer, C.D. and D.H. Romer (1994), "What Ends Recessions?", *NBER Macroeconomics Annual* 9: 13–57.

Romer, C.D. and D.H. Romer (2013), "The Most Dangerous Idea in Federal Reserve History: Monetary Policy Doesn't Matter", *American Economic Review* 103: 55–60.

Rohde, L. (2015), "Danish exchange rate peg since 1982", speech at Nykredit Capital Markets Day 2015, Copenhagen.

Rudebusch, G.D. and L. Svensson (1999), "Policy Rules for Inflation Targeting", NBER Working Paper No. 6512.

Ruge-Murcia, F.J. (2006), "The expectations hypothesis of the term structure when interest rates are close to zero", *Journal of Monetary Economics* 53(7): 1409-1424.

Sands, P. (2016), "Making it harder for the Bad Guys: The Case for Eliminating High Denomination Notes", M-RCBG Associate Working Paper No. 52, Havard Kennedy School.

Schmeidel, H., G. Kostova and W. Ruttenberg (2012), "The Social and Private Costs of Retail Payment Instruments", ECB Occasional Paper No 137.

Schularick, M. and A.M. Taylor (2012), "Credit Booms Gone Bust: Monetary Policy, Leverage Cycles, and Financial Crises, 1870-2008", *American Economic Review* 102(2): 1029-61.

Securities and Exchange Commission (2014), "Money Market Fund Report: Amendments to Form PF", Final Rule (issued 23 July).

Segendorf, B. and A.-L. Wretman (2015), "The Swedish Payments Market in Transformation", *Sveriges Riksbank Economic Review* 2015:3.

Shin, H. (2016), "Bank capital and monetary policy transmission", panel remarks at the "ECB and its Watchers XVII" conference, Frankfurt, 7 April.

Shleifer A. (1986), "Do Demand Curves for Stocks Slope Down?", *Journal of Finance* 41(3): 579-590.

Stock, J.H. and M.W. Watson (2007), "Why Has U.S. Inflation Become Harder to Forecast?", NBER Working Paper No. 12324.

Stock, J.H. and M.W. Watson (2015), "Core Inflation and Trend Inflation", NBER Working Paper No. 21282.

Summers, L. (2015), "Central Bankers Do Not Have as Many Tools as They Think", commentary in *Financial Times*, 6 December (www.ft.com/intl/cms/s/2/755a7cf6-9c34-11e5-b45d-4812f209f861.html#axzz45p24CjE7).

Summers, L. (2016), "It's time to kill the $100 bill", Washington Post, 16 February.

Svensson, L.E.O. (2003), "Escaping from a Liquidity Trap and Deflation: The Foolproof Way and Others", *Journal of Economic Perspectives* 17(4): 145-166.

Svensson, L.E.O. (2016), "Cost-Benefit Analysis of Leaning Against the Wind: Are Costs Larger Also with Less Effective Macroprudential Policy?", NBER Working Paper No. 21902.

Sveriges Riksbank (2013), "The Swedish retail payment market", Riksbank Studies, June.

Sveriges Riksbank (2015), "Swedish Financial Institutions and Low Interest Rates", *Financial Stability Report* 2015:2.

Sveriges Riksbank (2016), *Monetary Policy Report*, February

Swanson, E.T. and J.C. Williams (2014a), "Measuring the effect of the zero lower bound on medium- and longer-term interest rates", *American Economic Review* 104(10): 3154-3185.

Swanson, E.T. and J.C. Williams (2014b), "Measuring the effect of the zero lower bound on yields and exchange rates in the U.K. and Germany", *Journal of International Economics* 92(Supplement 1): S2-S21.

Tobin, J. (1972), "Inflation and Unemployment", *American Economic Review* 62: 1-18.

Ubide, A. (2016), "Central Banking since 2007: The Great Experiment in Monetary Policy", manuscript, Peterson Institute for International Economics.

UBS (2016), "Negative interest rates: The Swiss experience", Global Research, 7 March.

Wadhwani, S. (1986), "Inflation, Bankruptcy, Default Premia and the Stock Market", *The Economic Journal* 96(381): 120-138.

Wadhwani, S. (2013), "The Great Stagnation: What Can Policymakers Do?", Centre for Economic Performance Discussion Paper No. 1198.

Wang, Z. and A. Wolman (2014), "Payment choice and the future of currency: Insights from two billion retail transactions", Federal Reserve Bank of Richmond Working Paper No 14-09.

Williams, J.C. (2014), "Monetary Policy at the Zero Lower Bound: Putting Theory into Practice", Hutchins Center Working Paper No. 2.

Witmer, J. and J. Yang (2015), "Estimating Canada's Effective Lower Bound", Bank of Canada Staff Analytical Note 2015-2.

Woodford, M. (2003), *Interest and Prices: Foundations of a Theory of Monetary Policy*, Princeton, NJ: Princeton University Press.

Woodford, M. (2012), "Methods of policy accommodation at the interest-rate lower bound", Federal Reserve Bank of Kansas City Symposium, Jackson Hole.

Wu, C. and D. Xia (2015), "Measuring the Macroeconomic Impact of Monetary Policy at the Zero Lower Bound", Chicago Booth Research Paper 13-77, University of Chicago Booth School of Business (revised 2015).

Wyplosz, C. (2001), "Do We Know How Low Inflation Should Be?", in A. Garcia-Herrero, V. Gaspar, L. Hoogduin, J. Morgan, and B. Winkler (Eds.), *Why Price Stability?, Proceedings of the First ECB Central Banking Conference*, Frankfurt: ECB.